Teen

real teens

Diary of a Junior Year

volume 1

New York Toronto London Auckland Sydney
Mexico City New Delhi Hong Kong

ISBN 0-439-08408-3

Distributed under license from
The Petersen Publishing Company, L.L.C.
Copyright © 1999 The Petersen Publishing
Company, L.L.C. All rights reserved.
Published by Scholastic Inc.

 Produced by 17th Street Productions,
a Division of Daniel Weiss Associates, Inc.
33 West 17th Street, New York, NY 10011

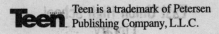 Teen is a trademark of Petersen
Publishing Company, L.L.C.

SCHOLASTIC and associated logos are trademarks and/or
registered trademarks of Scholastic Inc.

12 11 10 9 8 7 6 5 4 3 2 1   9/9 0 1 2 3 4/0

Printed in the U.S.A.   01
First Scholastic Printing, September 1999

Special Thanks to Laura Dower

The diaries you are about to read are real. Names, places, and other details have been changed to protect the teens involved. But what they have to say all really happened.

Who We Are

Marybeth <u>Miller</u>:
    I'm a wiseass. I can make just about anyone smile, even if they're feeling down in the dumps, and that's really important 2 me. Some days I consider myself fatter than others, but what are you gonna do, right? I run track and play basketball and keep on—so it's no big deal. Mostly I love just hanging out with my friends. Mom, Dad, and my brother and sister r cool 2, I guess. I mean, we don't <u>always</u> get along, but I pull thru. I don't think I would want anything else.
    <u>LIKES</u>: My yellow Polo shirt
    <u>DISLIKES</u>: People who can't take a joke

<u>Billy Shim</u>:
    I'm an outgoing, crazy guy, but I have mixed feelings about it. I'm smart and get good grades, but I know that's not good enough so I need something that stands out like sports, sports, sports! The scene with my parents is totally up/down. We have great moments, but we have arguments too—like good grades = heaven and

bad grades = hell. But my older brother Lee, who's playing football at college right now, he's always there for me. Lee is the nicest guy you could ever meet. I think things would be easier if I were more like him.

<u>LIKES:</u> Sports, sports, sports (esp. lacrosse in spring)

<u>DISLIKES:</u> Stupid, clingy chicks

<u>Teresa Falcone:</u>

There is much more going on in my mind than the eye can see . . . I love writing, reading, dancing, singing, acting, playing field hockey, listening to all kinds of music, and most of all being with my friends and family. I know I'm smart and get really good grades, but I have this problem, which is everyone sees me as this airhead. I hate that! Sometimes I can be sooooo insecure! My parents are divorced, so I live with my mom and my older brother Vincent, even though we don't get along ever. My dad lives a town away, so I see him a lot.

LIKES: Romance books and anything else romantic!
DISLIKES: Not being taken seriously!

Jake Barosso:

Ladies think I'm cute, but only sometimes. I'm shy, but I love to dance and I'm always on the go. I love raving, riding a Jet Ski, playing pool, and fixing up my new car. My dad is really really sick, so things are terrible at home right now, but I try to help out as much as I can. We're always arguing about the stupidest things. I wish it didn't have to be like this. I like to make Mom + sis laugh whenever I can. I'm funny too.

LIKES: My car!!!
DISLIKES: Being sick + people who are assholes (a tie)

Katie Carson:

I am involved in Community Club and student council, on the tennis team, and a peer ministry leader of my church, among other things. To fit it all into one word, I am well-rounded. My schedule is nuts, but I handle stress with my sense of humor. I have important long-term goals for myself. Sometimes my friends tell me I am naive about things, but I really do believe I have the ability to get along with <u>everyone</u>. The most important thing to me is family— we're very close and share a special bond. I can tell my mom everything.

    <u>LIKES:</u> Musical theater, travel, good grades, Brad

    <u>DISLIKES:</u> People who don't have any goals

<u>Edward Baxter:</u>

This is me. I'm all the characteristics associated with this picture. I love listening to music, watching TV, and playing Nintendo. I'm a yearbook editor, sometimes I run track and I'm in Community Club, even though I'm starting to hate it, and I mean REALLY HATE IT. I'm also a bad speller, but for the most part I do well in school. As far as parents go, mine

Who We Are

are like <u>big kids.</u> My dad is a real comedian and my mom is stupid funny, like me. My older brother Jerry is away at college.

   <u>LIKES:</u> Coconut my dog

   <u>DISLIKES:</u> People who never call you back, especially when you beep them

Emma West:

   I think I'm totally trustworthy, kind, and respectful, but if someone starts talking about me behind my back I feel a lot different and I get upset. At school I'm ice-hockey manager and I'm in community club and student council. I love hanging out but I usually don't make any plans until like the last minute, usually with marybeth. The most important thing is that my friends mean the world to me. my parents are cool too. They're always running around doing a million different things and my little brother Ronnie thinks he runs the house. my sister Lynn and I have to babysit for nim

Who We Are

a lot, which can be a drag but whatever.
<u>LIKES</u>: Having a boyfriend
<u>DISLIKES</u>: Being left out

<u>Kevin Moran</u>.
I'm all this. smart, funny, hyper,
and I don't know what else kind of
guy. I kinda go from one thing to
another like wave running, clubbing,
swimming, mainly any sport—and mostly
just chilling with my friends. Still,
I get bored all the time. My
family, they're loud, and Dad has
been married 2x so we have a lotta
freakin people here to deal with
and we argue like ALL THE TIME
but that's cool I guess cuz I
really do love them all. I was
really close to my sis Lena, but she
died like 8 years ago when I was 8,
which still makes me mad.
<u>LIKES</u>. Dressing and doing stuff
exactly as I want it and no one
can tell me anything else
<u>DISLIKES</u>. My brother Neil no
doubt!

Kevin

So I realized today that I really don't want to go back to school tomorrow for obvious reasons of homework and waking up early and all that shit. But *I DEFINITELY* want to see my friends so bad. This was the first summer that I was really homesick for them. I missed raves and hanging out and just doing nothing but doing it together. I don't think junior year is gonna be the same as before. I'm thinking that it might be kind of lonely this year, and one of my biggest fears is being alone. It's just not like it was being a freshman or even a sophomore. And there's going to be so much work. But I'm not going to make myself crazy like Katie.

Like tomorrow, I'm gonna look good and worry about the rest later, ha ha. Seriously, I got some new clothes on sale the last week of summer. I'm gonna wear my best outfit tomorrow: my JNCO khaki pants and Nike sneakers and a tuff tee. I was talking to Jake and he says he is gonna wear new rags too because he wants the girls to know he's available and I guess I do too. I want to find someone special this year. I'm sick of lame hookups. Ta ta for now.

p.s. Only 42 days until I drive!

Jake

September 8

One thing I know for sure is that *I HATE SCHOOL.* Today was the first day of junior year and I already know how bad tomorrow's gonna be.

Thank God for Kevin because he is the best friend anyone could ever ask for. He's the funniest, coolest of da cool guys in the whole world and we are like brothers, we are that close. He is really helping me out these days. He doesn't try to tell me how to run my life or anything, he just stays really cool and keeps me up.

I have my eye on this one girl and we were talking over the summer but I don't know what to do. Kevin says I should go for it as soon as I see her at school, and the truth is I was hooked on her from the day I saw her last year, but I don't think she knows that.

It's funny, when I was in middle school, I had so many girlfriends and guy friends but since we started high school all of those girlfriends have become sluts and have left me to go for older guys with cars.

Teresa

Sept 8

Dear Diary,

It's finally *HERE*—the first day of school! God, would I ever love to get A's in every subject this year but my downfalls are AP history and physics so maybe it's just not possible! They are my most unfavorite subjects. I need to get serious though, because I am a junior now and everything matters. Here's what I need to do:

Get better grades
Go on a diet!!!!
Be in a better mood at school
Open myself up to guys more
Go to states in field hockey
Write more poems!
DO SOMETHING!

Every year I do this, I make this list of everything I need to do and then I never do any of it. This year it's gonna be different, I know it. I have a feeling. I kinda need to change the way I feel toward school. I mean, I get good grades but my attitude sucks. I'm so motivated sometimes and then other times I don't study. What should I do? I have so many new goals and hopes and I am sick of sitting back and just watching my life whiz past me so I'm going to do something about it.

The other night I was reading a magazine and I found this horoscope, which I think describes me perfectly:

As usual, you start the school year with fantastically high energy and go-for-it spirit. Your urge to accomplish is huge! Your ruler Mars is giving you a megaburst of energy,

which explains why you're supercreative and brimming with ideas. But organization is the key. Take tips from a bud on keeping schedules and keeping study time productive.

FOR ONCE IN MY LIFE I would like to be able to say I did this and that I got it all together—grades, sports, and love of course!

Katie

September 8
@ 3:45 p.m.

I'm terrified about school. I loved being the baby for the last 2 years. Someone always seemed to be there to help me with homework and listen to my problems and just to take care of me! Now I have come to the realization that I have to take care of myself. Last year I kind of hid in the shadows of the upperclassmen, but this year is the beginning of everything for me. It's a lot of pressure. But I work well under pressure, right?

I want to do really really well in all of my classes this year. No exceptions. *I can't take ANY chances.* I feel like I've always been compelled to succeed ever since I was born. Mom says I used to lie in bed at night just saying over and over, "I have to learn how to read." I taught myself by memorizing words. Even though I was a little kid, I knew.

11

Last week I was busy running errands for school and everyone was making fun of me . . . teachers, students, everyone! I was planning out the activities for Community Club and student council for the whole *YEAR*! I can't believe it because it's so much to do in such a short time, but I did it. And I also ran frosh orientation. I gave a talk to all the incoming students about what they should expect at JFK when they start out and what changes when you move into the upper classes. The teachers on the orientation team at JFK told me that they were "duly impressed with the way I handled myself." I was very pleased.

Oh and I have decided that I'm definitely better at tennis since the summer, so I hope I'll move up on the team. I played almost every chance I got. Just as long as I can beat Rachel Ross, I'll be fine. She may be my teammate but she is definitely my best enemy.

Baxter

September 8

I don't know why everyone makes such a big deal out of junior year. I think it's just going to be like any other year. I'm a little concerned about my AP classes, but I realize it's better to face them now than at college. The thing I was most excited about today was seeing my friends again. I guess I saw most of my best friends over the summer, but school is the only place where you can see everybody in one place at one time.

Last week I had to finish all my summer prep work, like a 20-page packet for AP chem with 100 questions. I also had to finish reading four books for AP English. Actually I really only read three, but I think I'll get away with it. I also had to get my notebook, pencils, pens, homework pad, and labels all ready. Here are my classes:

Course Title		Credits	Teacher	Room
A006	Homeroom	.00	Alpert	025
B251	Italian	5.00	Helberg	311
C054	AP English	5.00	Sonstein	110
D449	AP Chemistry	6.00	MacTaggart	LAB
E419	Oceanography	2.00	Wallberg	107
F791	Adv. Photography	2.00	Gardner	DR
G137	Social Issues	5.00	Mullarkey	318
H343	Math Theory	5.00	Vozar	204
I452	Honors Physics	5.00	Cooney	LAB
J802	Phys Ed.	3.75	Franco	GYM
K812	Health	1.25	Morton	019

This bites. This year the schoolwork is going to be very very very very very very very very very very very very very very very very very very very very very very hard. I think I'm going to have like six hours of homework every night. There's a whole bunch of kids set up so we can call each other up for help, which makes me feel better, but I have already decided that when it comes to tests this year I study alone.

I can't believe it, but my parents are already

13

talking a lot about college. So I better make sure I do well—I have a lot to figure out.

Today when we were all eating lunch I was really thinking that everybody looks the same as last year. And there was Emma being so uptight about how everything had changed so much. She wouldn't shut up about it. I don't know what the big deal is. I really don't.

Billy

9-8

I saw Kevin, Jake, Baxter, and the rest of the guys at lunch today and it was cool because I didn't see them much over the summer. I have this weird feeling though since this year we don't have any classes together as opposed to last year when we saw each other like every single period. But I'm totally psyched for football. We only had a few practices over the summer, so I'm ready to get back into it.

Anyway, it's 11:32 p.m. and I'm getting set to call Blair D. She's my girl, I guess. Well, really she's just a hookup from over the summer, nothing too important. I don't know what to call her. She's pretty cute but I don't really feel like being exclusive. None of the other guys on the team are.

I was thinking that now that we're juniors, all these freshmen look up to us. Like Blair D.—she's a freshman too. I guess I'll just play along with it to see what happens. Maybe it'll turn out to be something more. Maybe not.

My brother Lee always says that you have to keep your options open, especially when it's only the beginning of something. He went to JFK too before he went to the University of Michigan. He was a running back on the football team and he won all sorts of plaques and awards. Lee is the kind of guy who does everything right and gets whatever he wants. Actually, he's the greatest guy you would ever want to meet, but he's a lot to live up to. My parents are always comparing the two of us.

Emma

9/8, 5:03 p.m.

I am so glad to be back to school since summer was really boring. My sister Lynn and I had to take turns watching our little brother Ronnie so I couldn't get a job or go out during the day. All my friends had summer jobs so no one could hang out with me while I was watching him. I did go down to the beach a couple of times, but when I really wanted to go I couldn't because I had to watch my stupid brother. Whatever.

I'm not looking forward to waking up at 7:00 every day, but I'm excited because it's my junior year and it's the most important year of high school. I didn't really do too much to get ready though because I was in California the last week of August and I came back like 3 days before school started so I didn't have time to do things. But I did get these new sneakers, which I love because they have yellow in them. I knew I wasn't going to get dressed up for the beginning of school so I wore my favorite jeans with this really cute gray tank top with like a frog on it and all these sparkles. I think I looked pretty good. But it's not like anyone was looking at me.

It was bad enough not having much of a love life over the summer, but now coming into school and having to hear about how everyone hooked up really stinks. I personally would never do it, but some kids I know cheated over the summer. Anyway it seems that *EVERYONE HAS A BOYFRIEND OR A GIRLFRIEND* to talk about except me. They're all making plans and me and Baxter are the only ones who don't have someone special. Whatever. Tomorrow I will wear my other new top with the blue flowers on it. Right now I'm gonna call Marybeth so I know what she and Sherelle are up 2 this week. They said something about hanging out at the Silverado tonight but I don't know if they decided to go or not.

xoxoxoxox, emma

Marybeth

September 8th
People say we're supposed to enjoy the teenage years because they're the best days with no worries

and no "real" problems. Well, to tell you the truth, I think whoever said that and whoever believes that fell on his head. Don't get me wrong, I love high school, but it really is tough. I also think it's harder being a girl too. I don't think there is any girl growing up right now who isn't questioning herself. Whether it's in their looks, their weight, or how well liked they are. Ok, personally, I don't know if I am or if I'm not, but there isn't a day when I don't look in the mirror and feel kind of disgusted by what I see.

I can't really say so for sure since I haven't got a clue about what it's like to be a guy. But Kevin says it's *EXACTLY* the same for guys. They don't have a clue either! Even though we haven't been hanging out so much together, I think I still trust Kevin more than *ANYONE* else at JFK.

I know that now as a junior I am on the "upper half" of the totem pole so I'll get more respect, but people can be unpredictable too. Sometimes it can be hard to tell who your friends are and who gets all wiggy now that we're getting older. But I won't be down. The whole negative scene is so un-me. If I'm having a feeling fat day, it's hard, but what are you going to do, right? Just laugh about it. Even though I'm not crazy about what I see when I look in the mirror, I wouldn't change my life for anything. I'm not desperate about anything. (Ok, I have done a few stupid things in the past but we'll ignore that for now.) All in all I'm trying to roll with the punches, and I do have the greatest friends.

Maybe now that I'm 16 I will finally get my tongue pierced (in my mother's nightmares but I *REALLY* wanna do it!). I've been talking to Sherelle on the phone and she says we're in for a bad year (as in a *GOOD* year). Getting into trouble is sometimes worth it, so we'll see. We can do some serious damage this year if we put our minds to it!

Billy:

JFK High School is very diverse, especially the junior class. We have punks and idiots on one end, and then normal people in the middle—not like crazy or dumb or smart, just average. Then there's the smart end, which is basically me and all my friends.

Teresa:

Just ask anyone: I hate cliques, and our school is VERY clique-ish. I used to cry all the time here because I thought I didn't fit in anywhere. Just ask Kevin about that one. But now I think my grade is pretty awesome.

Baxter:

Our grade gets along just fine. What's the big deal? Even though everyone doesn't hang out, everyone is always cordial to everyone else and whenever there is an activity dealing with us, we always come together and do a decent job.

Emma:

Our school is like a typical high school. The junior class is good, I guess, except for when people gossip and talk about other people, which they do a lot. I hate that but whatever. It's cool when everyone gets together at games or just hangs out at lunch.

Jake:

I HATE SCHOOL. Except auto shop. That's the best.

Marybeth:

My school is ok 4 me. I'm basically friends with everyone.

OurSchool OurSchool

Kevin:

My class is odd, kind of, cuz there are like sooo many separate groups of people. Everyone tries to get along and it isn't bad but it IS too weird, like everyone is separated from one another. Plus my school is like cutting back on programs and that really sucks for me and a lotta other kids who wanna do stuff.

Katie:

JFK is a small high school in a small town where everyone knows everyone else's business. As much as I hate some aspects of being here, I must admit that it isn't all that bad. See, at JFK, it really is possible to be the star of everything.

Teresa

Sept 10

I can't wait to turn 16. I bet everything is different after that. I'm already planning my Sweet 16 in my head. My mom is letting me have a huge party and she's renting this hall. It is going to be soooo excellent with a candle lighting ceremony and everything. This is how it works: you pick 17 different people that represent your life and they come up and light the candles on your cake while you read a special message for them and play a song dedicated to them. It's really 16 people for your age and then one extra for good luck. I already know who I want to light my candles.

Jake

September 10

Starting junior year has been way easier with friends around, especially someone special: Claudia. We started going out yesterday, September 9, when I asked her at exactly 4:23 p.m. I've been talking to her for about a year but she was already taken before now by this asshole Jon. What a total loser—I think maybe he fooled around on her but I don't wanna think about that. She looked so beautiful today. I can't even describe how lucky I feel right now. This weekend will rock because love is awesome. Claudia is awesome.

Katie

I am so lucky that Robert is out of my life and Brad is in my life. I can't believe that when I first met Brad, I thought it was just a meaningless crush. Well, I didn't really feel that way deep down inside. (I've had enough hookups during my singledom to know that this was different, that he was different.) Brad is such a gentlemanly person and so sweet—nothing like everything I was used to with "the animal" Robert.

I just looked at the picture on my dresser of Brad and me taken down at the beach a couple of weeks ago and he looks so sweet. He has the best eyes. Just thinking about him makes my heart beat like a clock.

I can't wait to see the look on Rachel Ross's face when she finds out that Brad and I have hooked up. She'll die all over again—worse than she did last year when Robert and I dated! Only this time maybe she won't stick her ugly nose into everything. She is such a total B@&%$ when she's trying to dig up dirt! If she only knew the truth about the fact that everyone secretly hates her including me, then maybe she wouldn't always act like Miss High and Mighty all the time.

Marybeth

September 10th

I can't believe it but I am already beginning to feel kind of overwhelmed by school this year even after only 3 days. It's weird. I talked to Kevin about it and we agree that *PEOPLE HAVE CHANGED*. Some old friends don't get what's going on with other friends and vice versa. It can be really awkward sometimes. It's not always that people change (I take that back I guess), but more like the bonds between us are changed. Like me and Katie used to do stuff all the time (and she and Sherelle were way tight too) but now it's like we're going in 2 completely different directions and we are leading 2 completely different lives. It's bizarre.

I've been thinking a lot about how different our friendships were last year and even more different the year before. When we were freshmen and even sophomores I was so close to Katie, Kevin, Jake, Emma, and all the others from our group. Now it feels like none of us will be hanging out except maybe me and Emma since she, me, and Sherelle are girlies 4-ever. And of course then there's Greg.

I saw Greg after school today, which I didn't really expect. I have to admit that I'm dreading the thought that I might not be able to see him as much now that school has started (since we hooked up a lot over the summer), but I'm hoping that'll work out too. We're talking about going to the football game in two weeks with Sherelle and her steady guy Bobby. Greg and Bobby are football buddies so we'll probably spend a lot of time this fall going to games and hanging out at some drinking parties or whatever.

Kevin

Oh yes, going *back to school SUCKS* just like I thought. Big surprise. This is like the longest first week of school I can remember in a long time. I saw Marybeth today and she said the same thing, ha ha (she is definitely my BFF). I can always have a heart-to-heart with her and when I do need advice on a girl or on my life, like my family or trouble when I'm down, we keep each other informed. I can get mad and shit and she doesn't even care.

I just cannot believe how much Chemistry class *REALLY SUCKS* this year! My teacher is already coming down on me and we've only just started! I really don't know how much more of this I can take—it's like I want to slam him into the chalkboard, and feeling that way is just not like me. I am not a violent person.

So far this is what all my classes are gonna be:

25

1st period, Advanced Algebra

2nd period, Gym

3rd period, chemistry honors — SUCKS!

4th period, Comp. Lit

5th period, Honors Spanish

Lunch!!!! Yeah

6th period, SAT Prep 1st semester
            but then Auto Shop 2nd
            semester. Yeah

7th period, modern history (this is a
            pretty cool teacher)

I really was dreading getting a shitty schedule and not having any people that I liked in classes with me but it's kinda decent how it's worked out. Except for Chem. Mr. MacTaggart is totally a pain in my butt. He does not even know how much we make fun of him and he is so 100% impossible to understand. Yeah, and in the meantime we're all *FAILING*! But of course then there's math which is *REALLY* the hardest—like, stop already!!

I'm gonna work hard and do good on my tests and all, cuz this is the hardest year. Maybe Katie is right after all. I should just try to jam on my grades a little bit more. I'm gonna try, whatever good that'll do.

p.s. Hey, I forgot to mention I have definitely decided to ask Adina out. I've liked her for a while, but I like her more now than I did last year. She looks hot, and for some reason she's being sweet to me. I saw her the other day and was kidding around and she laughed. It's a good sign—yes! Stay tuned.

p.p.s. Only 39 days until I drive!

Baxter

September 11
You know, I take back what I said a couple of days ago about how junior year is the same as last year, because it really isn't after all. It kind of surprises me, but I hate school so far this year. Okay, I know it has only been a couple of days, but I can tell these things. Throughout my entire life I always loved school and did good in it. Now, for some reason, I hate it. And at the same time I really hate being like this. I think I'll go play Nintendo 64.

Marybeth

September 11th

Friday night and we're psyched! Me and Sherelle are going to the Silverado to meet up with some of the guys from the football team (yes, Greg will be there and I have the coolest boot cut jeans to wear with my phat boots!). I think Em will be coming too, she usually does.

Actually, it's kinda awkward already this year with Emma and parties and get-togethers and stuff. Me and Em will always be BFF, but some people I know find her kind of annoying. I don't, but other people invite me to parties and not her. I usually try to find ways to bring her, but she can be kind of a 3rd wheel, it's true. It's just that she likes to go where I go. Sherelle and her are pally, so it's usually not a problem. It only gets weird when Sherelle's boyfriend Bobby is around cuz he's one of the ones who doesn't like hanging with her. Maybe he would like Emma better if she had a guy and there were 6 of us?

No matter what happens, the truth is that those 2 are my girlies 4 life. There really isn't much I can't say 2 either of them or do 4 them without saying n e thing . . . so I just have to figure out the rest and not get hung up on who's w/ who.

Emma

Sometimes I feel so insecure and I feel like people are talking about me behind my back. I can tell when people are only joking around but sometimes it really bothers me. Out of all my friends sometimes I know I am the one people pick on the most. They don't mean what they say but sometimes I just get tired of it. I feel jealous because all my friends seem so happy. Everyone's already got a boyfriend or girlfriend, or they're hooking up with someone. I mean my friends deserve it, but I do too.

Katie

September 11
@ 8:27 p.m.

I've decided that I should spend most of this Friday night trying to get my life organized before the school year really starts to take off. I swear that my life has been so nuts lately that I've had to type a new list for myself on the computer almost every morning in order to keep everything straight and make sure that everything gets done.

Today Kevin was complaining about schoolwork and I don't really get it. It's only one year of major focus on grades. One year! Why is that so hard for people to deal with?

EVERYTHING MATTERS WHEN YOU'RE A JUNIOR.

Today I was also thinking how lucky I am that JFK is practically my second home and I will always love it and keep it close at heart. I actually have a master key to the school. The administration trusts me and I spend more time there than anyone else in my grade doing work. Having master keys also comes in handy on a morning like this morning. In the rush of new classes and everything I escaped to this old closet that was converted into an office for Community Club and student council. It sounds kind of dark and dreary, but it has two skylights and it's soundproof (I think it was a sound studio once too) so the rest of the school is blocked out. I can go there if I just need to escape or think and get stuff done. I honestly don't think anyone knows I spend as much time there as I do, but I go in and out as I please. I guess you could call it my special place, although a few times I hung out in there with Baxter.

Five Goals for Junior Year

Baxter:
1. Get better than 1300 on my SAT,
2. Get a girlfriend!!!!
3. Get straight A's
4. Get a nice car
5. Win a trip to Australia

Emma:
my license.
a good guy.
Good grades.
Good college.
I dunno. not much else.

Billy:
1. Keep my A average or else
2. Find a hot girlfriend
3. Get new friends that fit me better
4. Pass my driver's test!
5. Get 1st team All-Division

Five Goals for Junior Year

Teresa:
1. I hope I can bring my class rank up from 5 to 1!
2. Find the right colleges to apply to!
3. Have a 4.0 GPA or close to that!
4. Be field hockey captain — Go Bulldogs!
5. Be elected senior class president!

Kevin:
1. ok grades
2. stay with my special person (Adina)
3. keep all my friends
4. not change who I really am
5. accomplish all my goals

Jake:
1. Get good grades
2. Get a good job
3. Play good in lacrosse
4. keep raving
5. keep Claudia

Five Goals for Junior Year

<u>Katie:</u>
1. Maintain a high GPA despite AP classes
2. Move up in class rank to 1, 2, or 3
3. Get a lead in JFK musical
4. Get nominated for a position in the Intrastate School Committee!
5. Stay organized!!!!!!!!

<u>Marybeth:</u>
1. Try a little harder
2. Care a little more @ school (I get good grades but it doesn't matter much b/c I don't care a whole lot)
3. Party w/o getting caught
4. Don't let others influence me
5. Definitely appreciate more of what's going on around me. Nothing specific, everything in general.

Jake

September 11

I came home today from school and my dad is getting worse and I can't stand the pain. Within the last year he has gone from the greatest man to a great disabled man. He has this disease called Becker MD. It's this muscle disease and he's just getting weaker and weaker. My mom says that we should try to make everything normal and act like nothing is happening, but I'm sorry, I can't do that. I think as you live your life, good luck evens out with bad luck and now I am in a bad luck phase. When I was younger I had it all. I thought I had a great family, money, toys galore, a beach house, and all the great friends I needed. But we had to sell stuff for money for my dad to get treated and I don't have as many clothes as I used to. It's like slowly my family is falling apart. Everyone is always fighting and I try to stay out of it but it's hard. I try to help out sometimes but I can't. My father wants to help too but he can't, and he gets sad and starts crying and that's the worst. I guess I need to spend more time with him, but I also want to live a normal life.

marybeth

Something is definitely up with Greg. We've been going out since the middle of July, which is cool. But now all of a sudden he's starting to get "funny" w/ me. I mean he only calls when I beep him and stuff. Well, yesterday he called Sherelle and told her his feelings for me had changed. He says he doesn't know what he wants and he still doesn't want to lose me either. I think boys are cracked. And Sher told me everything last night. Now I'm a total *wreck*.

That is why *LUV SUX*. You only know how much something truly means to you until you're about to lose it. I can't believe this could happen to me. I am embarrassed too, like we probably should have just broken up over the summer and kept it like a summer thing only. What am I supposed to do now? I didn't think *THIS* was gonna happen. Well, I think I have to call up Greg even though I don't know exactly what to say.

God, love sux so bad. I wish I wasn't going out with him at all now. I wouldn't have tried to see him so much. And here I am all worried about what he's gonna think at parties like I'm cheating on him. Oh well. I never did anything bad against him, did I?

I feel so gross inside. I don't want to do anything right now. Maybe I'll call Kevin first. No, I am putting this diary down right now and calling Greg—there is no stopping me.

11:22 p.m. same nite

I called Greg and he was actually there and we talked. God, I am still nervous but everything's back to the way it was again. I guess before, like over the summer, we were just friends with benefits, and now he was talking to me like I was the most important thing that had ever happened to him. He was saying he needed me back in his life completely and told me I needed to trust him and all that. So now what do I do?

Teresa

Sept 12

Dear Diary,

I just found out from my guidance counselor that I am starting the year as #5 in this class of over 282 kids at JFK. How awesome is that? I am so proud. My mom said we could go get our nails done to celebrate. I am determined to do *EVEN BETTER* this year. I am so glad we moved here a few years ago. I mean, I haven't been in this school as long as everyone else, but this place is soooo much better for me.

Katie

I guess by now everyone has met Brad, even though he doesn't go to JFK. I don't know what everyone really thinks about him cause I never really get a straight answer (except from my Mom who *loves* him, or so she always tells me). I hope everyone likes him—it matters to me, even though I know it shouldn't. He really treats me well—better than I am used to! Better than Robert did, that's for sure.

It's funny how it works, Brad is like my complete opposite but he slows me down when I am over-loaded. He is so much nicer and he isn't possessive in the same way Robert was at all. I sure would like to keep him around.

When I think about Brad I get homesick for the summer. We had such a good time at the beach in August. At first we would go to the boardwalk with friends and do cute things like he'd put his arms around me and all that, but it still wasn't going to that next level. Then all of a sudden one day it happened. After months of just talking, we had our first kiss . . . August 9th . . . and it was the most awesome romantic experience of my life thus far. Brad had come down to my parents' beach house for the day with a few friends and we were riding jet boats in the bay. Anyway, the two of us were on the wave runner by ourselves so we were absolutely alone. But this was the first and last

37

time I was going to let him drive it—he broke the boat! He threw us off so far and so hard, in this mucky area, and I just went nuts! As he was pulling me to the boat, which had landed like 50 feet away (there was no way I was putting my feet down), and I was yelling at him, he just picked me up right there in the middle of the water and kissed me. It was amazing—like nothing I'd ever felt before with Robert.

Baxter

September 13

I'm watching last week's episode of Buffy on tape. I know it's not good to watch TV all the time, and I don't really do that, but there are some shows that are totally unmissable. And Sarah Michelle Gellar is so hot I can't stand it.

My dad, being the big comedian of the family, just told me to go outside today and rake the leaves. Now THAT'S funny! There's absolutely no way I'm dealing with the backyard today. I was kind of hoping Katie or maybe even Billy would call today, but so far nothing. I hate feeling left out. I wonder where they are? This is pretty boring but at least it's not as bad as school seems to be working out. It's terrible. Maybe I'll call Marybeth since she's always good for a laugh. I swear, she is like the funniest person I know, and no matter what I always feel better after talking to her.

Marybeth

September 13th

My old buddy Chris went back to college and it *SUX*. I am gonna miss him so much. Sometimes it really scares me but I think I'm sort of in love with him. Only Emma and Sher know that though.

I felt kind of bad for Baxter today cuz he called up feeling really out of it. Poor kid. I had him laughing though, and I felt like I had done my good deed for the day. That's how it works for me, I like to find someplace or someone I can cheer up when they're down in the dumps. It's like I can usually sense what someone is thinking before they know it, like I'm reading their thoughts. He's a good guy though, even if he does tend to get a little uptight about stuff.

Baxter told me he was gonna blow off running this year but I told him not to. Last week I went to see the coach about signing on for track again this year too. I'm not sure if I want to go for basketball again though. I still need time to decide.

I think maybe I'll send an e-mail to Chris just for the hell of it. Tell him how much I miss him already. Then I'm ready for bed. I stayed up 2 late last nite w/ S + the boys.

My Perfect Saturday Night

Jake:
   A night at the phattest club playing the best house music, with Claudia in my arms and my friends all around me.

Emma:
   I never know what I'm doing on Saturday night until like 5 minutes before I do it. I get on the phone with my friends and we try and decide. Normally we just drive around. Then we go to the 7-Eleven to see who's hanging out there. Then at like 11 we all go to the Silverado Diner for a large cheeseburger with onions and a Coke. Sometimes we go to the mall, but we always end up at the Silverado and do whatever.

Teresa:
   I'd go out to a club dancing with Sherelle and some other girlfriends, meet a few hot guys, then go home and have a _huge_ all

My Perfect Saturday Night

girl sleepover and band all nite while stuffing our faces.

Kevin:

First me And my boys JAke, Micky LAzlo, And Jonny All get shit-housed on vodkA, my fAvorite drink. Then we go clubbin And I dAnce. Then we go on A CARibbeAn vAcAtion And everything keeps getting better. Of course, AdinA would be there too And we'd hook up.

Katie:

I'd spend the day shopping (I live for it), then have dinner in the city with Brad and all my closest friends. Then we'd see a musical (another thing I live for).

Billy:

I'd try to look really sharp and then take a girl out to eat at a nice restaurant, then maybe go to the mall and catch a good movie and then get together with her.

My Perfect Saturday Night

Marybeth:

It doesn't really matter what I do, as long as it's fun and I'm with my BFFs.

Baxter:

All of my friends and Jessica (I wish so much) come over to my house and we just play Nintendo or watch a movie and talk and laugh down in my basement.

Emma

So it's Sunday night, a typical night at home and everyone is just hanging out. I dunno, my mom is still cleaning up a little bit and my dad said he was tired, so he's lying down and Mom's upset, but whatever. We're gonna have dinner soon I think, but Mom doesn't feel like cooking as usual so we're just waiting for spaghetti or whatever she throws together. Mom is talking about how Dad is not doing anything to help her out around the house but I don't think he is really listening. They do this a lot.

Anyway, I'm not feeling as good as I was yesterday and that's since I hung out with everyone (Marybeth, Sherelle, Bobby, and Greg) at the Silverado last night until like 12 a.m. It was a little weird being with them—I don't really know why exactly.

I wish I would get an e-mail from Cliff or something. He's this guy I like from the other side of town. We've known each other for a really long time, but anyway we're just talking for now. *NO BIG DEAL.* We still haven't hooked up.

Of course, hooking up is just one of many stages everyone goes through in their relationships. First you're just "talking," which is spending some time, then you move on to hanging out together, then you hook up, which is like making out, and finally you get hooked up, which means you can't

43

see other people except the one you're hooked up with. And that's also called "being together." And technically you can still "hook up" with other guys if you're still not "hooked up" and "together" with anyone.

I wish something would happen soon.

Kevin

9/15

The best thing that could ever ever happen to me happened today and it is the *BIGGEST DEAL* and that is the fact that I went on a date with Adina. Yes! She is beautiful, a true genius (literally), she is so sweet to me and she's really cute. *FINALLY SOMEONE!* I never knew last year (she was a freshman then) how great she was and I am really glad to be realizing this now. I am so surprised and happy. Maybe this will be a good school year with someone I care for. I have a good feeling this could last.

Plus—only 34 days till I drive!!

Teresa

Sept 16

Dear Diary,

Kevin is getting his license in only *ONE MONTH*— oh my God, I am soooooo psyched for him! This year is *SUCH* a new beginning for us—thank God! In so many ways last year was absolutely the *WORST* year of my life but things are looking up every day. I think a lot of what I was stressing out about last year was the opposite sex. No matter what I do it just seems that *I CANNOT FIND THE RIGHT GUY*. I mean guys aren't everything, but they do add a special touch to your life. I guess I'm just a hopeless romantic. I feel like wherever I go I'm noticing who's in a couple and who isn't and that makes me feel a little weird. I mean it's not like I think there's anything wrong with being single but still I really just notice who's paired off.

Kevin

9/16

FANTASY #1: I take Adina to the beach and have a romantic Saturday night with the one I love in my arms. We watch the sunset and chill with our wine (very romantic), watching the moonlit sky in pure heaven.

I want my first time to be truly memorable. I really want something special. But on the beach too because I love the water soooo much and I am mystified by the beauty of the sunset and the waves rolling in on the shore and the moon. It's perfect.

It's funny how no one really knows this part of me, not even my mom and dad. That I'm completely like sensitive and romantic (I love shit like that). I'm great and feeling ok with everything so far. I wonder how long it's gonna last?

Now only 33 more days until I drive!

Teresa

Sept 16 late

Dear Diary,

Every time I see people on TV kissing or I hear about the cute little things boyfriends have done for my friends, I get soooo jealous! No one has ever really gone out of their way for me, but I would love for it to happen! Then again I haven't really ever had a long relationship. Maybe someday. It's partly my fault because I do have trouble settling down with one guy and even if I end up with a good guy he usually screws me over. Oh well, I get so impatient with guys. All the good ones are taken! Like Kevin, who is totally one of my closest friends. People always have said that we would make an awesome couple and we've agreed more than once to try to work things out, but it has never worked, and that upsets me a lot because in my eyes he is the closest thing to perfect.

9/16
mad late

I can't sleep and maybe I'm just being paranoid but I feel like everything inside me is getting ready to *EXPLODE* like all at one time and I dunno what I'm supposed to do except sit here and wait for it to explode. All I can think about is Adina, but also it's like a picture of the end of the world inside my head. I don't know why I am feeling all apocalyptic and shit, but I just am. Sometimes I think that writing in my diary is just such a stupid thing to do and it gets boring or just annoying cuz I think I should be talking about my views in here and not just the day-to-day shit. But then again the days are going by and so much is happening it's all a part of those same views. I feel like I have my own idea about how life should be and how I should act.

Sometimes I think it's all because of what happened to my sister Lena. I get all weird and angry because she died so young. I was just a little kid and she was 16, but I miss her and I get angry at how unfair everything is.

Like how I feel about religion. I have this whole shpeel about it cuz I believe in God and heaven and all that, but I just don't understand sooo many things about how life is and why life is. I've witnessed and experienced a lot of traumatic times in my own life (like Lena) and I don't understand sometimes how there is a God. How can he just be sitting back most of the time watching us suffer as human beings—die, fight, and basically do everything that destroys the world? It's like why are there so many people with misfortunes and disabilities if he is all powerful? Why not make all people happy? To me this whole life just seems like a sick game sometimes and we are all in a dangerous place. How could God have let my sister die? Of course Dad doesn't ever talk about feeling this way. He wrote me a card once with these words on it and told me to think about them always:

ALTHOUGH THE WORLD IS VERY FULL OF SUFFERING,
IT IS ALSO FULL OF THE OVERCOMING OF IT.

I want to believe that. I try to believe that. I think of it all the time especially when I remember Lena. My dad really is one of the greatest human beings anyone would ever want to meet. He has the biggest heart I have ever seen in my lifetime and if someone is in need he'll kill himself to help them out as much as possible. And I know that's what life is about. I just wish it didn't have to hurt. Ta ta, Kevin

Teresa

Sept 17

Dear Diary,
    I was thinking more about Kevin and me hooking

up and I realize that every single year we really have tried to work out something romantic. Why hasn't it worked? Like freshman year he liked me for a while and then we were both down at the beach for Memorial Day weekend and were together the whole time. Then he also liked me during sophomore year but I didn't know about it, and then I decided in the middle of that year that I liked him too, but he didn't know and that was the end of that.

I was thinking about how now Kevin is dating Adina and there probably won't be a chance for us to get together in junior year. I'm really happy for him and all, but it makes me sad to think that we're missing this golden opportunity or something. Of course, Adina is all Kevin talks about and she seems incredibly sweet and I really really *LOVE* her so much, but I'd be lying if I said I can't help but feel a little left out. It's really hard for me to accept it (he doesn't know I feel this way, he would die if he knew). I also hate the fact that she's beautiful. But he's my close friend and if he's so happy, that's what matters and I'm happy too. I am mature enough to accept this (I hope).

Billy

9-18

Is Blair D. just in love with me for the license I'm going to be getting in a month? *YES!* I swear the girls go more for the guys with cars. Anyway, for some stupid reason all I can think about is Blair D. And she's not even really that hot. Is it worth getting together with a freshman? What will my friends think? I'm so tired right now. The only way to revive me is music and a Coke. A nice cold glass of it. Junior year is a mess already.

I can't believe that this weekend I have homework for a chem quiz, Spanish, and an AP prep test. But like all the high school students I know, I procrastinate. I probably won't even crack open a book until Sunday night. For me, studying so early in the year is the biggest grind. There's homework and more of it. And what about football practice? If it weren't for my English teacher, Ms. Gifford, I would be getting to sleep at night during the week at 11:00 p.m. instead of at 1:00 a.m. It's crazy. Here it is Friday and all I really want to do is go to sleep.

Kevin

9/18 Friday

The best thing that I ever coulda done was ask Adina out cuz we are really having a kick ass time together! She looks so awesome and today I noticed she was wearing these cool-n-funky shoes. Tonight we swung by the Silverado to catch up with Marybeth, Sherelle, Teresa, and everyone else. Of course no one really goes there until late on Fridays and we were there way earlier than everyone else so we didn't stay long. I despise that stupid diner anyhow because whenever you go into the Silverado Diner you come out smelling like bad hamburgers. Later on Adina and I just hung and watched the stars. She said she liked the way I was wearing my hair. As everyone knows I have odd ass hair and sometimes people think it's wack. But not Adina, she told me she liked it unique, even if I bleached out the tips (which would be weird since my hair is black). Later she wasn't feeling so good so we called up her dad and he picked us up right away at 11. I can't wait until I have my wheels so I don't have to go on dates when it's convenient for parents and not for us. Nothing is worse than that.

p.s. I'm getting my license in only 31 days!

Katie

September 18/19
Friday @ 1:38 a.m. (well, Saturday)

I can't sleep.

One of the kids from one of my summer programs called me today and wanted to know if I wanted to go out with him. I thought that was a little weird. I told him no nicely, that I have a boyfriend, and he was okay with that. I'm generally so suspicious of guys now since everything with Robert last year.

I'm finally getting rid of most of my anxiety over

Robert. When I was first dealing with the fallout of our destructive relationship at the end of sophomore year, I didn't want to feel or talk about anything, and I definitely preferred that my friends not know all my feelings on certain subjects at all.

Now things have really flipped around, but when I think back to last year I keep wondering. What happened?

Freshman year at JFK I came into the school like this shy scared frosh that had a low profile during all of middle school. I immediately threw myself into my studies and into tennis. After being extremely successful in both, I began to draw myself out of my shell. . . . That's when I became involved with Community Club and student council. I formed all these important bonds with key teachers and role model upperclassmen who really influenced me so much.

Of course one of these "role models" was Robert Williams. He was accomplished like me, or at least that's what I saw: he was in Community Club too, starred in all the plays, Managing Editor of the school newspaper, etc. In my freshman naivete, I must have overlooked the fact that he didn't have too many friends and that my friends on the baseball team called him "wussy" because of his lack of athletic skills. I just thought they were being juvenile calling him that and paid no attention. What I saw was the benefit of having an upperclassman boyfriend (especially being a frosh) and the image that the two of us would have in the school, to the faculty, especially. I needed to make a strong impression.

Our relationship went well for the first couple of months or so, but then when I went away for the summer after freshman year and when I came back as a sophomore, I don't know what I was thinking staying with that jerk. Like when we started school that year he was suddenly so possessive of me. If I achieved ANYTHING he was jealous of it, jealous of anyone who spoke to me, or congratulated me, or wanted to hang out with me. What was I thinking?

He went from being overly protective to verbally degrading. It was abusive, I know that now. I can see it looking back, but at the time I was like, "How did I get here? What am I doing wrong? Why is he being like this to me?" I just want to block it out. Especially since Robert didn't stop with just words. I can't believe I let Robert hit me.

Enough about Robert. I'm putting on a surprise birthday party for Jake tonight. I thought he deserved something special, especially with his father being so sick. I hope I can get some sleep before then.

Baxter

September 19
Now this is so weird. I was at the movies today with some of the guys and we saw *him*, Robert, that evil guy from Community Club that Katie was to-

gether with last year. He's such a *PIG*! Kevin was there and he said he was going to beat his head in if he talked to us. Kev gets pissed like that sometimes. It's a good thing Katie's ok now.

Anyway, I'm going to see what's on the WB. They have some really good new shows. Then I have to get ready for Jake's surprise birthday party. Katie's having it, which was really nice of her.

Jake

September 19

Tonight I had the surprise of my life. My friends all threw me a surprise birthday party and I loved it. I had no clue what was going on and I was actually a little scared when everyone jumped out at me and screamed. But it was the greatest night of my life. Most of my friends were there and my girlfriend Claudia was too. She and I had an ice cream fight—it was so funny.

The only thing missing was my dad. I wish that he could have been there too to see my excitement, but he was home watching TV. I wished on the cake that Dad would be cured one day so that our family could go everywhere and do everything with him like we used to. I miss him and I know my brother and sis do too. I miss the days when we could play soccer and walk around together and he could fix the flat tires on my bike.

Thank God for my friends, especially Kevin. I don't know what I'd do without them.

Katie

September 20
@ 12:38 p.m.

Jake's party went really well. Everyone had a great time and even helped clean up. He was thrilled. I guess it doesn't take that much to make someone really happy.

My brother and sister, Paul and Patti, are watching TV and I just got off the computer. Here's my to-do list for tomorrow (Monday):

Don't forget tennis practice (bring camera)

Need to outline student council presentation

Volunteering News article coming soon

Spanish project

Prepare for church retreat!

There is a TON to be done!

I am a little overwhelmed by my school/tennis/volunteer schedule, but my life is crazy as usual and I have to just get used to it. I was just cleaning out my backpack and even though I am trying really hard to be organized, I am soooo disorganized (already!). I hate it! I am constantly carrying around too many books and other things because I am just too lazy to store stuff in my locker. I bring more to school than anyone else—I am always dragging something like 3 bags around with me. (But as my mom says, at least I am always prepared!) One time last year I remember it was really cold in the classroom, like 30 degrees or something, and I pulled out this big bulky sweater that Gran knit for me, which I just happened to have in one of my bags. Of course some of the other kids made fun of me for it, but I think they were just jealous because I was so prepared. And they were freezing!

I have so much work that I have to give up things like the phone and some nights I don't even get to talk to my friends or Brad. Well, they say that success is measured by what you have to sacrifice in order to achieve it.

Oh, I saw this in a book somewhere and I love it even though I am not usually into this stuff:

> The man stood on the high cliff:
> "Come to the edge," he said.
> "We can't," they said. "It's too high."
> "Come to the edge," he said.
> "We can't," they said. "It's too high."
> "Come to the edge," he said.
> "We can't," they said. "We'll fall."
> "Come to the edge," he said.
> And they came, and he pushed them,
> and they flew.

The Nicest Thing Anyone's Ever Done

<u>Jake</u>:

It just happened. My friends planned a birthday party for me and I was psyched.

<u>Teresa</u>:

My friend Stephanie brought me a card, soup, and a stuffed animal when I was really sick. That was soooooo sweet!

<u>Katie</u>:

Last July the group from my summer school program threw me a party in the college dorm where we were all staying and everyone had such a good time. I had no idea it was going to happen! I was so touched.

The Nicest Thing Anyone's Ever Done

Baxter:

The nicest thing is when people just call just to talk for no reason. Not calling to ask "what's the homework, Bax?" They just say, "what's up?" and start talking about life. Marybeth does that a lot and I appreciate it. She makes me feel good.

Marybeth:

When my friend Rick takes me to Burger King, and then we spend the day together. We do nothing, but we have so much fun just being w/ each other.

Kevin:

I get bACk A lot of rEAlly niCe things cuz I try to put out, being niCe to othERs All the time. YeAh, And my fRiENds help me when I'm down And listen to me And All thAt. No one pERSon moRe thAn Anyone else,

The Nicest Thing Anyone's Ever Done

but reALly JAke is the one who
listens the most.

Emma:

  Last weekend my friend Sherelle
brought me a yellow friendship rose. I
thought that was the nicest thing. I
wasn't expecting it at all, especially
from <u>her</u>.

Billy:

  My dad's getting me my own set of wheels
and the girls will love that!

Billy

9-25

I just had this weird feeling about being back in school like it's two sides of the same coin. It's great because I personally feel a lot more power and respect from the lower classmen and even the seniors above me. I feel like I have gone through two years of hell and heaven and nothing can stop me now. But it's also like every day is a step closer to losing my friends and that scares me. I only have 2 years left with these friends and that is pretty hard to deal with. I mean, what happens when you go on to college? Are we just wasting time getting stressed about work and grades and looking good when really we should be paying more attention to these people who we'll never be friends with again? I look at my brother and he really doesn't talk to his high school boys much except when he comes back to watch football games at JFK or comes home from U Michigan for the holidays. What is it?

I saw Baxter today before I left for the game and he's stressing out about school too. Why can't we just figure it out? He did help me out today though by giving me some homework answers when I didn't have a chance to do the assignment. I didn't want to get in trouble with my Chem teacher. So he really came through, which was cool.

Baxter

Billy really pisses me off sometimes. He constantly degrades me and makes fun of how I look, how I act, how I talk, and my family too. If I do better than him on a test he makes fun of me. And if he does better than me he rubs it in my face. But I think I know why he does it. I think he's jealous of me and my family. Billy really doesn't have a close relationship with his parents. They never go to his football games and they didn't go to his play either last year. Where on the other hand my parents go to every single one of my track meets. But according to Billy track isn't a real sport, of course. He would say that since he's a football player. And nothing else I do after school counts. He thinks all I do is watch TV, and since he plays football he makes me feel worthless. I really hate that.

Like today I gave him some homework so he could copy it, and while he was copying my homework he started making fun of me again. Billy's a good friend and all, but sometimes he can be a real bastard.

I'm kind of pissed at Emma and Jake too. I was supposed to go to the football game with Emma but she never met me and now she won't call me back. Then I talked to Jake earlier and he said he would call me back, but he never did either. That really makes me mad. I am constantly trying to make plans with other people and no one calls me back. So I am stuck home on a Friday night, mad at the world. I don't know why I don't tell people how mad it makes me. I guess I just feel like keeping the peace.

Jake

September 25

I can't stand it when people think they know you and they just don't. Hey, I'm not gonna tell you how to live your life, so don't tell me how to live mine. Baxter left me this message tonite about how annoyed he was with me because I didn't include him in my plans. That was like out of the blue completely. I didn't call him back because I didn't know what to say. I didn't even go anywhere that special. I just went over to Mick's place with Kevin and some of the rest of the crew.

Tonight sure was a huge switch from last week for sure. My surprise party was so awesome and it felt so good to have all my friends around me. But now things don't seem to be going so well. My dad especially. I wish he would get better soon.

Kevin

9/25

I'm psyched cuz I'm getting my car painted for cheaper now and it's a phat paint job—jet black w/

some purple and blue in it. Definitely sweet though.

Um, tonight was pretty cool—it always seems as if we aren't going to do anything and most times it isn't any good, but times always end up okay with my friends. Jake and I went to my boy Mick's place and played pool and chilled. It was Jake, Mick, and some other kids plus Adina—that's what made it sweet.

Today she put a card in my locker that explained our whole pasts and how it is with us now and how I stole her heart. It made me so happy. I really think that she and I can go places cuz she is the only one who has ever done anything sweet back to me. No one I've gone out with has made me feel like this. It's like she can read my soul or something. Then tonight when we were at Mick's house she looked at my keys and asked me how many keys did I have. Me thinking normally said 2 (the truth), and she said nope there's like one more invisible one and she meant the key to her heart.

I wanted that moment to never end.

Only 24 days until I, Kevin Moran, drive! Yessssss!

Katie

September 26
@ 7:23 p.m.
Mom says her heart hurts and that makes me so sad. She's really tired from my sister Patti being sick all

summer, and now she's even getting a little bit worse. She's got problems with her blood and she's been sick a lot this year. Mom and Dad are so strong though. Last night Patti didn't feel so well and so my parents took her to the hospital and stayed there until after 1 in the morning. They look pretty tired today. The doctors had to give Patti massive doses of morphine for pain. She's had like 3 different kinds of tests and transfusions in the past 2 months. It makes me feel so bad. She and I used to fight all the time but now things are much better between us. I said a lot of extra prayers for her today.

Brad's grandfather is pretty sick right now also. Brad and his family are having a hard time with it. But he and I try to share everything from triumphs to sorrows, and I am always listening to him if he's upset and he is there for me to spill everything (and I mean everything), which is just what I need sometimes.

Next week Patti has to go in the hospital again so I told Brad to remember how I get sad when that happens (just in case I explode in some weird mood out of nowhere). I like to warn him about stuff like that. Even when I want to be in control of situations, I can get emotional. But it's okay to talk to Brad about my bad days or anytime I'm upset. He just rubs my back and makes me feel better.

Teresa

Dear Diary,

I'm feeling a little blue and I don't know why. *WHY DO I FEEL BLUE?* I wrote this poem today. I am so glad I decided to be a poet because it's like the best way to express myself, even if I am the only person to read these.

NEEDING SOMEONE

I have been given spirit,
I have been given delight.
I have lived in a place
Where life always seemed right.

I am a believer
And I believe I should love,
There is no room for hate
I should try to rise above.

Through trials in my life
I have searched for some clues,
And I've experienced things
That give me the blues.

I admit I have lived
With most things I need there,

Like family, support, and
Tender loving care.

But needing you is a trial
Like I have never known
Needing you is a hardship
When I am all alone.

I need your special words,
When you say you're all mine.
Why can't you just do that?
Won't you send me a sign?

Though I have love in my life
From my family and friends
Until I hear you say "I love you"
My heartache never ends.

Love is so confusing! I am a true believer in signs
and symbols that things are meant to be. Sometimes I
saw things with guys in the past that basically made
me think they were the "ones." Now I just don't
know. I have given up on looking for that long-term
relationship. I think I'm the only one out of all my
friends who has never had one. That's weird, right?
What is WRONG with me? Am I doing something
wrong? I'm giving up trying to figure it out.

In some ways I think me & Kevin are soul mates
if there is such a thing, and maybe someday we will
be together. Of course not right now, since Adina's

around, but maybe some other time? Then again I think maybe I have given up my search and want someone to seek ME out rather than the other way around. Maybe I just have a real problem because I confuse friendships with guys with liking guys, and that's maybe something else I need to figure out.

But I'm not going to let guys walk all over me, cause they tend to be after one thing and that's *SEX*! That's all they ever think about. That is for sure. And you have to play hard to get with guys because the minute you say "I like you" or show major interest, *BOOM*, they're gone! My friend Josh actually says that he goes for girls who play hard to get because it makes them more attractive. Can you imagine? Those are the rules of dating according to guys. I find that disgusting.

Baxter

September 28

There is one girl that I sort of like. Who am I kidding?? I feel like I'm in love with her. I have been constantly thinking about her since the beginning of school. I don't know her that well, but she is a year younger than me and she plays soccer. Anyway, her name is Jessica Glazer.

Well, today I fell in and then out and then in love again. I saw Jessica giving a big hug to this other sophomore Ed so that kind of broke my heart. So then I started flirting with her best pal Megan. Now I have a crush on *her*. Hopefully this one will work out.

Today I asked Kevin what I should do about Jessica and Megan because I know that he gives the best advice even though I usually don't take it at all. My hugest problem is that sometimes I tend to over-react. He told me to keep cool and see what happens so I guess I will do that.

Billy

9-29

I don't know how I'm going to get my homework done. I forgot we're playing the 8th best team in the state this week at Grimes. Huge game for us. Hope we win!!! That's all that's on my mind now, not school. Oh, and Blair D. too. I'm always thinking about her.

Katie

September 29
@ 9:13 p.m.

I was thinking today that there is really no one else like Baxter in the whole world. He shares my values. Bax and I are so different from everyone else at JFK, which is comprised of one too many cliques of all kinds—the nerds, the football players, sluts, and so on (really!)—and I think we're the only people who really have the ability to get along with everyone. In the past two years so much has changed. A lot of kids have turned to drinking and sex to get through, but Baxter and I just won't, I know this for sure. We're too involved and have too much going on to ruin it, and one drink, one sip of beer could ruin everything. Reputation is too important to us. We have ranks to uphold. I am in positions of leadership in which the teachers, principals, and administrators look to me to set examples for the rest of the school. Sometimes I am sure that Baxter and I are the only ones who understand these values. We generally keep what we're thinking between us. Baxter jokes that I have an "in" with all the teachers and that no matter what I do I can get my own way. Actually, it's true in a way. I'm not the kind of person to take advantage of a position like that. But it won't hurt my college applications either. I know it sounds impossible for a teenager to say this but *REBELLION IS JUST NOT AN OPTION FOR ME.*

Baxter

September 30
Katie really pisses me off and I can't even defend myself! For whatever reason she always compares me

to her and tells everyone how alike we are. We are not alike. She thinks that I can't draw just because she can't. She thinks that I'm not artistic because she's not. And now I know I can't trust her with my secrets.

I should have never told her about Jessica. She constantly brings it up and that is annoying enough. Now Emma told me Katie passed her a note in class about it, about me and Jessica. Thank God, Em ripped it up. Come on! Grow up, Katie!

The thing is I don't even know if I like Jessica anymore, as if anybody cares! I just want to like someone who likes me. So if Jessica doesn't and Megan does I will be just as happy, that's all. I don't know why Katie had to go and manipulate the whole situation, like she knows me better than I know myself or something. She can be such a controlling person. I really hate her for this.

Katie

September 30
@ 4:51 p.m.

Sometimes I think that high school is just about getting good grades and getting into college, and lately I have been feeling so much pressure about that. I guess I don't really know where I want to go, but I think Stanford sounds cool and Harvard, of course, will be on my A-list. Then again, I know it's all a game and the chances are that I may not come out a total winner. My heart thumps just thinking about applying, and I know I will be so stressed out.

I can't help but think how many other Kathryn Diane Carsons there are in the universe and how many of them will definitely get into Stanford over me. I have so many decisions to make, but I can't help but feel that in a lot of ways it's way out of my hands. I can't control everything even though I want to. Is that such a terrible thing for me to want?

Marybeth

September 30th

Come sta? (means "How are you?"). Italian class was boring because I was tired today for some reason. I told my pal Chuck that Emma said hello to him and he got all weirded out by that. I think she's gonna write him a letter but maybe not. She doesn't know if she wants him or not. Aaaaaaaaah! She's a little hard to figure out these days. I don't know what she's thinking a lot of the time. *WHAT DOES ANYBODY WANT?*

I talked to Greg last night on the phone and it was the first time in a long while that our conversation was actually pretty good. I'm beginning to think that everything is going to be ok with us, which I am happy about. Later tonight I'm going out drinking with Sherelle, Bobby, and a bunch of other guys.

Katie

Right now I am at the tennis championships for our county. I haven't been on the courts yet but I'm really nervous about playing, something that rarely happens. My partner Gwen and I have to play one of the best teams in the tournament, and it's going to be really tough so I am dreading it.

I was at church last night. I have always looked at religion in a funny way, but lately I have been having more faith somehow. I can't explain it. I guess it is just part of growing up and finding myself.

@ 11:24 p.m.

Oh no! We lost in the quarter finals (oh well). In the first match we played today I sprained my ankle pretty badly too which was part of the reason we lost. I can barely walk around and that is frustrating me. I have to suck it up though, cause on Monday I have to play *again*!

Brad heard I'd hurt myself playing tennis and came over to the courts to see me and see how I was feeling. He did! At that point I had a bag of ice on my ankle and I was on a chair wrapped in a blanket watching my pal Gwen play her singles match. Brad was like a godsend. I was feeling kind of down in the dumps and he just sat down next to me and rubbed my back and comforted me.

I have to admit that it was really fun to be able to show him off to everyone there since the last boyfriend of mine that they knew was Robert, who was only like this short nerdy guy who looked more like he was 14 than 17. Brad is totally different. He is like tall, black hair, green eyes (those eyes!), and he is definitely hot. My friends and even my tennis coach were saying that he was hot and they were congratulating me. Eat your heart out Rachel Ross, he's mine.

Ever since my ex-boyfriend Robert, Rachel is obsessed with hating me and doing anything she can to spite me. Unfortunately I still have to see her at tennis all the time. This is the person who used to hang all over Robert when he and I were dating, and there was nothing I could do about it. She actually admits that she's applied early decision to college so she can be at the same school as him. I can't believe she ADMITS that! She was friends with Robert but he certainly would never have gone out with her, not for a minute. He told me that once.

When Robert and I broke up, at first there were all these crazy rumors all over school about what happened and why we broke up, and people were taking sides. Like people actually came up to me in school and asked all this personal stuff about what happened! All the guys on the football team were ready to kill him. But what did Rachel do? She sided with HIM and got really mad about the fact that people were degrading her "man." Huh? I swear she blames me for all the bad rumors about Robert that were spreading around. But I didn't do anything. I was the one who was in the abusive relationship!

And then as last year went on it only got worse. I beat her out for the lead in the school musical and I won Community Club election over her only friend (nobody likes Rachel, why would they?). I was asked to do the solo in choir—stupid Rachel was rejected from that one because she can't really sing anyway! And of course this season my new tennis partner and I have been playing *MUCH* better than Rachel and her partner.

I'm younger, but it's me who is successful and she just can't handle that. She is soooo cocky about *EVERYTHING* and she has no right to be. Once she retaliated against me by kicking me off the Debate Team because *SHE* was the co-captain. Now that was really low! Last year when prom came she didn't have a date and she was sooo pathetic that she actually went with her cousin from Canada. What—she can't find someone in her own country? She is such a B&$#%! I don't hate many people, but I don't hate anyone like I hate her.

I know I get a little carried away but once I start talking about how mad Rachel makes me feel, I can't shut up.

Teresa

Dear Diary,

   I just found out today that one of my poems is going to be *published* in this anthology of lots of other kids' poems! I am soooo excited. My mom took me out to dinner to celebrate. This is the poem. It's called *Falling Apart*.

FALLING APART

I see a big door
In my dreams every day
I want to go in
But something blocks my way

A force holds me back
And I cannot go in
There's a voice in my head
Saying "you cannot win"

My parents they say
I must pass through this door
A door to my future?
Tell me, what is it for?

If I am to enter
I must be wise and sure
Are there things to be done?
Help me unlock this door

I will love, I will trust
I will cherish my friends
Are there things to be done?
Yes, beginnings and ends

And when I know what it takes
To open my door
I will travel through
And let my life soar

The door of my dreams
My mind and my heart
My life opened up
No more falling apart

—T.J.F. 8/27

Jake

October 1

Claudia and I broke up. We've only been going out for like a month but we've been talking for about a year and I am in love with her. She said she just needs time to think about things. Hopefully we are going to get back together. I miss her a lot already. I guess I need Claudia because it is fun to be with her and I can tell her all about my father and everything else. I hope she decides she wants to be with me.

Marybeth

October 1st

Greg is a total loser. I don't really mean that, but we can't seem to figure out what's going on between us. It's so weird. Like last week he was not answering my calls. Then he acted like such a total jerk to me and now all of a sudden he's cool again. Tuesday night this week he was a real jerk again and I told him. It was mostly because I was in such a bad mood since Chris went back to college that day and I was so sad. But since that Tuesday, things have been great! Greg really means so much to me. Like we are so alike, yet we are completely different. I dunno. It's weird but we connect.

Then of course there's Rick Wright. He wants me too, but I'm totally into Greg. I think Wright's nice. We hang out a lot and stuff, but it won't ever be more than friends. People are starting to say stuff to us as if we're together, but *WE ARE NOT TOGETHER.* Like Emma thinks I lead him on, but she is way wrong. I don't lead him on, do I? I'm just playing. I don't know. Maybe.

I guess that's all for now. Except that I heard from Kevin that Jake and Claudia are busting up, which is terrible.

Kevin

10/3

I feel really bad for Jake. He's so upset by this whole thing happening with his girl Claudia needing some time alone. I don't know what to tell him anymore cuz truthfully even though I want them to get back together, I don't think it will happen. Even if they do there will always be the fact that no matter how much she likes him it won't compare to how much he loves her. She just can't ever catch up.

There is another reason why I think it won't work, and that is because she hooks up with a lotta guys. I just don't think she's ready for something special. I think that maybe Claudia has been hanging around her ex-boyfriend too much. Some people I know say they've seen her at his place lot. He's so messed.

I really hate her for screwing with Jake's emotions like this. He and no other guys deserve to be treated like this. I just wish he could find someone he likes who's good to him. Personally, I think he and Teresa would be really good together. They're friends and it's not like they have ever hooked up or anything, but whatever.

p.s. I'm getting ready cuz I'm having a big birthday bash and I'm inviting *EVERYONE* I can think of. It won't be a drinking party or anything, but it'll be great.

Only 16 days until I drive!!

Marybeth:

When someone pretty much completely changes to be like their new b/f or g/f. Also when a friend backstabs you and tells something you confided in them to the whole world. That sux.

Jake:

When a guy gets a girl and blows you off or if a person you like ends up being a real asshole.

Teresa:

When friends do things with you out of obligation, not because they really want to. It's so fake and so obvious.

Kevin:

Getting too much into A physicAl or like A love kind of RelAtionship with someone. It could wind up reAlly messed up AfterwArd.

M e s s U p a F r i e n d s h i p

Emma:

When they ditch you and don't call and act like everything is normal afterward.

Baxter:

Using me for homework. I can't stand it if someone copies from me and takes all the credit and then they look smarter.

Katie:

Betrayal. Good friends are always there for you through the good times and bad. A friend should come before any new boyfriend. I've seen so many friendships ruined over relationships that didn't last.

Billy:

When people take advantage of what you have, like a car or good grades.

Emma

Last night I was a little upset with my friends. Marybeth came to the football game with my cousin and me because she didn't want to go late and she said Sherelle was going late. Well, we got to the game and everything was going good. Then when it came time to leave, Marybeth decided to go home with Sherelle and not me because they had plans to do something after the game. They told me I could go with them, but I felt bad leaving my cousin, so of course I couldn't go. Sherelle told me to call her when I got home and I did. But of course she never called me back. Whatever.

It just really pisses me off because I feel like they always leave me out. Sherelle and Marybeth are always doing things together and I just feel stupid when I hang out with them. I dunno. Me and Sherelle got into a huge fight a couple of days ago because she thought I was mad at her. Me, Sherelle, her boyfriend Bobby, Marybeth, and this kid Rick Wright all went bowling and I told them I didn't want to hang out with the four of them because I felt stupid. They all like tell secrets and don't include me. That makes me really upset. So at the bowling alley I didn't really say much and Sherelle thought I was mad at her. Then later she wrote me this huge e-mail saying all this crap about how I should tell her if I'm mad. Whatever. I guess I don't really care. I can't stand it when she pulls shit like that. I mean I guess things are ok and she is my best friend but sometimes we do fight and I hate it.

Teresa

Dear Diary,

There's going to be this big Community Club rally at Red River next week and I was just thinking how maybe I'll meet someone there. It's like an opportunity to meet some new guys from the area or something. Hmmm. I have to think about that one some more. Also, I got off the phone with Stephanie and *ONCE AGAIN* she has blown me off to go with her boyfriend. What's up with her? She said that he got tickets for them to go to a play for their anniversary or something so I guess it's ok. But she keeps doing this so it's getting real old, real fast.

Katie

October 3
@ 8:45 p.m.

Community Club had a regional training conference this weekend and 200 people from all over the state came to JFK because we were the host school and club. We'd been planning this forever.

I was put in charge of registration and with like 200 people to check in I turned into a total machine. "Name?" was about as much conversation as I had to spare. All of a sudden some kid comes up and says, "Paul London," and I almost lost it. He's this beautiful kid I was *IN LOVE* with for three years during middle school. What a weird coincidence. I felt little butterflies too, which really surprised me, especially since I'm with Brad.

Paul couldn't believe how much I had changed and grown up and he kept saying it to me over and over. And we have so much in common! Just like me, he's really involved in his own local Community Club. I honestly don't know how he recognized me because I look so different now. I was such a baby three years ago, I swear! Anyway, we exchanged e-mail addresses and we'll see each other at the Red River Theme Park rally next week. That's the Great Fall Rally for Community Club and I can't wait!

@ 9:30 p.m.

Brad just called—he went over to someone's house and I think everyone was drinking. Except him, I don't think. He maybe drinks a little bit, but not too much. Because of his size, one or two beers doesn't really hurt him. I hope. Drinking kind of scares me.

I really don't want to get attached to Brad because of what happened with Robert. But what am I supposed to do? I have feelings for Brad now that won't go away. But even if I can't really change my feelings, they still scare me, and I don't want that to affect our relationship.

Sometimes I think we'll have to break up and I'll have to go through the beginning and middle and end and everything all over again, like starting from scratch in a way. Is it just my fear that's getting in the way? I don't think I will ever get past it. I know it's so important to take risks. I just have to follow my heart no matter how much it scares me. I sure hope my heart knows where to go.

Marybeth

October 4th

Last night Greg called me & he was high. He was *SUCH* a jerk. I think it's time that I yelled at him or something when he calls, but I am *NOT* calling him first. For some reason *I ALWAYS FIND THE JERKS,* like I'm a magnet for assholes. But somehow I put up with it. Usually it's me who apologizes anyway.

I think I have a cold. My nose is runny and I'm sneezing. I wrote to my bud Chris at college a couple of times tonight. I just miss him so much I can feel it inside. We're just friends, but in my head I'm always comparing all of my boyfriends to him because he treats me so well. Whoever gets him is a lucky girl, that's for sure. He's the friend *EVERYONE* should have.

Katie

October 4
11:40 p.m.

Happy Anniversary to me & Brad!

I am about to keel over because today was so long, but it was so nice at the same time . . . and it had a fantastic ending!

I got up at 7 (after going to bed at 1:30 or so) and my knees were bugging me. I was in charge of this local Seniors walk-a-thon to raise money for the Senior Center. It wouldn't have been so bad, but of course it rained! I was shoved to the sidelines and the event organizer asked me to help figure out who came in when on this little computer.

After that, I had to see the college counselor for 2 hours (college!) and a Community Club get-together at 4. I went to church too somewhere in there and did homework a couple of hours ago. Then at 9:30 I answered a call from Brad, who said he was coming over in 10 minutes. He was acting strange and I was completely baffled. I put on a coat and waited outside . . . and waited . . . but no Brad. About 25 minutes later (he is ALWAYS late), he pulled into our driveway and dragged me over to the trunk of the car. Inside the trunk he had hidden a dozen long-stem red roses. I could have fainted on the spot. He is so sweet. He said they were for our anniversary and I couldn't believe it. I hadn't even remembered. When I was with Robert we never celebrated anything, but Brad always wants to have a party for something. Anyway, who else has a boyfriend who brings them roses? Not Rachel Ross!

It's so sad that Jake broke up with Claudia. I thought they were so perfect for each other.

Emma

10/5; 4:53 p.m.

Today was a pretty easy day at school for a Monday. But all us juniors have to take HSPTs—High School Proficiency Testing—this week starting tomorrow. How fun! I really am not in the mood to sit in a room for two and a half hours and take a test on reading, writing and math. I know how to read, ok? And if we don't pass we don't graduate high school.

Today at lunch these two girls got into a fight and they were yelling back and forth at each other until a teacher broke it up. That's okay though because this one girl is a freshman and she deserved to get beat up. Well, I mean no one *deserves* that but she is such a slut. I really hate her even though I'm really not a mean person. But she is going out with someone who is just too old for her and that really bothers me! Oh well, what is my problem and why do I care what she does with her life?

This lady just called me and asked me to babysit and I hate babysitting for her kid. The kid just cries and cries and it always ends up being like all day even though she says it's for just a few hours. I feel bad for her though. She has to go back to school at night. I'm only doing it because I could really use the money. Money never hurts and I won't have too much homework to worry about this week because of the tests, so I will do it. Whatever. The phone is ring-ing—I gotta go!

xoxoxoxoxoxo emma

p.s. I just talked to some people and found out that same freshman girl is going to be suspended or something. Of course that could just be a rumor.

Kevin

10/5

I've been getting pretty upset lately for some rea-son—I don't know why. I tend to think too hard about shit and then I start crying a whole lot.

Two of my friends are in the middle of a huge fight at school, over this asshole who's a real player guy. He's a senior who thinks he is *all that* and I dis-like him very much. There's Pam who is in my grade and another friend, Elaine, who's a freshman, and this jerk is lying to them both and manipulating the other when he does. Like he's dating Pam and tells Elaine he isn't. Then he told Pam he wasn't talking to Elaine. So now the two girls hate each other and not this player, which I can't believe.

All I keep thinking about is why does my friend Pam always end up with a guy who screws her up so bad? Why does that have to happen? I hate seeing anyone in pain, especially my closest friends. I had to see her cry so many times in misery over guys like this and here she is *AGAIN*. Anyway, I am really worried because someone will definitely get hurt physically and mentally over this. I don't know why this shit has to happen.

I do know though that it is good to cry—it lets you get things worked out that you need to get worked out. If someone doesn't cry he should, especially guys, because you can't hold on to everything—it's too hard. I learned that when my sister Lena was killed. But I don't want to go into that right now. My head is messed up enough.

Gotta get my HSPT testing beauty rest, ha ha. Ta ta. Only 14 days until I drive!

Marybeth

October 5th (at nite)

Well, I just finished painting my nails this bluish color. Looks pretty good only they're too short. Today I had to take those stupid HSPTs, standardized bullshit tests. That definitely was not cool. I don't run track tomorrow so maybe Greg will come over. I dunno though because we're sorta off and on now.

Today in class Sherelle sent me a note with a picture of a bear on it. It is so cute! Sherelle really is my BFF. She's convinced that Emma hates her, but I said she was wrong. Also, she said me and Greg are a great couple and should be together forever. . . .

Yeah, I dunno about *that*.

Emma

10/5 really late

Marybeth called me so late tonite (luckily my parents didn't wake up). Anyway, Sherelle thinks I'm pissed off at her again, which is like *whatever*!! Sherelle even sent me an e-mail about it! What is her problem?! I just don't want to care one bit, so I won't. At least I'll try not to care until it makes a difference. God, I better sleep if I'm going to take those stupid tests tomorrow.

Katie

Why is everyone so worried about the HSPTs? Today we took the reading section and it was a piece of cake. But the math section killed me. I am lost in that subject—it's my weakness. I cut early morning gym because I felt so exhausted, but otherwise it was a normal day. We had another tennis match, which wiped me out completely. I played singles and our team has literally played a match every single day for the past 3 weeks. I am so tired, but I still won because the girl I was playing against came from a less fortunate school and I swear she had never taken a tennis lesson in her entire life.

Rachel Ross was playing against someone who was equally as bad as my opponent. But here's the difference between Rachel and me: she takes advantage of the whole situation and creams her opponent. I was not about to go out on the court and show off my 5+ years of lessons like she did. My coach was really proud of me. Even if I looked like a 10-year-old out there, I still won 6-0, 6-0. And I did it the right way, unlike Rachel. Why pick on someone who's not as good as you, right? That will just make *ME* look bad.

I can't believe that last year Rachel was my doubles partner and that we took 2nd in the county championships together even though we *HATED* each other. You would think that because we share a lot of interests (like tennis, music, acting, Community Club, chorus, and other things) that we'd get along better. But *NO*, she is always so competitive with everything.

Jake

October 6

Today was kind of fun. I took the HSPTs this morning for school and it was sooo easy. We did nothing in our other periods either, just sat and talked. After school I went to Vito's for some 'za with my buddy Mick. We go there like every day after school. Everyone who works there is cool. We love it. We ate and then I went to watch my little sister Jill at this gymnastics meet at school. She's gotten real good at the balance beam since last year. She can even do a cartwheel dismount! Her friends are so stupid though because they always flirt with us and it's kind of cool but embarrassing at the same time.

Then we went to play pool at Mick's house, which I also love. I rock at pool. Kevin was supposed to come too but he didn't feel good. The truth is I think maybe he was just with Adina instead.

When I went home my mom asked me if I wanted McDonald's for dinner and she let me drive with my permit. I love Mom. She is so nice about that stuff and treats me to good food all the time. The only bad thing today was my older brother Nate, who is a total asshole to all of us. He causes so many problems and was arguing over something incredibly stupid. It makes my mom cry, and usually I'm the one who has to cheer her up because I'm the joker in the family. It's like what Kevin and I do—we make people happy. It's our mission in life.

Emma

10/6; 11:03 p.m.

You know, love really sucks! A lot of people say that teenagers don't know the meaning of love. That's so not true. Let me explain why I say this today.

After the HSPTs, I went to see my ex-boyfriend Chuck where he was playing soccer. Chuck can't play because he is hurt and he's on the sidelines, but I still went. Well, he was with his new girlfriend and she is *SO UGLY* (like really—I'm not the only person who thinks this). Back in 7th grade me and Chuck went out for a while, and it was so great. Then during the summer he decided to like another girl and so we broke up. I was upset and cried for a week. Then the girl he dumped me for cheated on him and I was so happy because he could see how I felt. Well, when 8th grade started out I was still like in love with him, and he still liked me too, so we started going out again. Things were great and people thought we were the greatest couple and we would never break up. We went out all year until May, when I broke up with him for being too jealous of my buddy Greg (who Marybeth was so into this summer). He hated the fact that me and Greg were good friends. Then freshman year I had a new boyfriend and thought nothing of Chuck for over a year.

But here's the thing, at the end of sophomore year I started liking him again, and during the summer we hooked up a couple of times. That meant the world to me. Now I think I love him and I can't stand to see him with another girl.

This summer at a carnival, only a week before he started dating ugly girl, he won me a stuffed animal and now I sleep with it every day. And if he finds out I'm talking to another guy he still goes crazy. My friends tell me he says things just because he knows I want to hear it. Every time we talk on the phone or at school he constantly makes fun of his own girlfriend to me. And I get happy when he trashes ugly girl, but I guess maybe my friends are right. Maybe he's just saying what I want to hear. He told me that he would always care about me and that I never had to worry about it. That meant a lot to me, but now I wonder if he was just saying that too.

Today at the soccer game ugly girl kept giving me dirty looks. I swear. Chuck says she's worried that he'll come back to me. Whatever. I wish it would just happen already. I wish he would tell me that he loves me again because he knows that I still love him. I wish things could just go back to the way they were. Oh well, I don't feel like talking about this anymore.

Teresa

Dear Diary,

This year I am really down on guys altogether. I was just talking to Jake about this because he says he's down on girls too since he and Claudia broke up. Actually, I'm the worst one because I pass around notes and say nasty comments about guys at school. I can't help myself. I really do have such animosity for the male gender. Besides, they've treated me badly and what's good for them is good for me!

But as far as a good friend like Jake is concerned, I'll go easy. With his dad being so sick and now Claudia going back to her ex, he's got it pretty rough these days.

Actually, Kevin and Jake are like two of my best guy friends in the whole world and I should learn from my relationships with them. Unfortunately, whenever I try to have something with a guy like them whom I trust, it just doesn't work out. Why is that?

WHAT IS WRONG WITH ME?

When Jake was dating Claudia, I kept thinking

how awesome it would have been to double date. Me, Kevin, Jake, and Claudia. The four of us! But then of course Kevin and I never really gave it a chance as usual. So it never happened. I guess I'm forgetting that one for good. I have to. Okay, I admit that maybe I still have a little bit of hope.

Now that I look back at what I have been writing maybe I am *MUCH* better off without a boyfriend for a while.

Anyway, I've gotta go over to Katie's to watch Dawson's Creek with some other kids. We do that sometimes. I think Kevin's going tonight, with Adina of course, which is cool (really it is!), and Jake and some others maybe.

Jake

October 7

Well, I took the writing part of the HSPTs today. It's so stupid. During the test me and my friends Jonny and Kurt were bored. They give you this writer's checklist and we started to draw these stupid faces like all over it, which cracked me up. Jonny's drawings were really the best ones. He drew a picture of me saying "Keep Raving" because I love to dance and *rave!!!*

I really did nothing after school because it was raining. I've been thinking a lot about Claudia, but I think I'm gonna have to try to find someone else. I love her, but I guess it's just not meant to be. I just don't know why I can't find the right girl.

A few of us are going over to Katie's house to watch Dawson's Creek and some other shows on TV tonight. I just beeped Claudia one more time. I really want to talk to her so I punched in a 911. I hope she calls me back.

Emma

10/7, 10:12 p.m.

I am in such a bad mood right now and I don't even know why. Well, I have a stupid chemistry test tomorrow and I don't even feel like studying. I mean I looked stuff over but I don't give a crap whether I pass or not. I have an A+ in the class so one bad test grade isn't going to hurt. Whatever. The teacher is kind of a jerk but he likes me so there won't be any problems. Earlier today I was driving with my dad to go and get my sister and he yelled at me. He didn't think I was going to stop at the light but I was. I was! He's been letting me drive with him in the car, only he gets nervous no matter what I do. It really pisses me off. *MY FOOT WAS ON THE STUPID BRAKE* and like I hate being yelled at because it just makes me more nervous than before. I was nervous the whole rest of the way home.

Katie

I was just watching Dawson's Creek and I think it's so popular because we can relate to exactly what everyone on the show is feeling. Last night was the season premiere and Dawson thinks he's just friends with Joey who has grown up all her life with him, but then he gets jealous when this guy asks Joey out and Dawson starts to think maybe there's more going on beneath the surface. I can relate to this completely. Like Brad and I were friends first and then something else just clicked between us. And in the show when Dawson and Joey decide to try going on a real date, they have this awesome first kiss. That first impulsive kiss was so truthful!

Joey's sister tells her that you can't necessarily trust the first kiss because it's only passion and that it's the second kiss that really counts. That's the one with sense behind it. And that is so true too, right? I can totally relate. I remember the first kiss being so wonderful and then afterward it was like, hey, what happened here? I was already analyzing everything. Sometimes I feel like I am such a hard person to understand and that no one really gets what I am about. Then when I see that on TV I wonder if maybe I am really just like everyone else.

Jake

October 8

Today I was thinking some more about what I want from this year. I only know one thing for certain. I love auto shop. Every day I wait for that class because it's the best. I can fix cars and now I can drive cars. What else can you ask for? Mr. Duffy is also the best teacher. I have my own car and I'm putting in a radio system and I'm gonna put in a La Bamba horn.

School is a little better than usual these days. But as far as home goes, my father is not doing that well and it's killing me. I miss Claudia more than ever too. She is just the only one who understands me. I don't think any of my other friends understand how much pain I go through everyday with my family and my dad.

One Thing My Parents

Emma:

They don't know sometimes where I'm going at night. Like sometimes I go to parties and don't tell them.

Billy:

My parents don't know how mature I really am. I'm really independent, but they treat me like a baby. If they knew how I am when I'm out by myself at nite, maybe they would see the responsible and mature side and just lay off.

Marybeth:

They don't know how I see myself sometimes, which is fat.

Kevin:

They know About drinkin And girls, cuz my pARents ARe cool About pARties And shit. But there is like soooo much my pARents don't know About whAt's going on in my heAd. They don't know how bAd I still feel About my sister's getting killed And how Angry thAt mAkes me

Don't Know About Me

inside. And they really don't know how sensitive I am.

Katie:

My parents know everything about me.

Baxter:

That my friends are constantly joking and teasing me. It's no big deal, but I think it would bother my mother a little.

Teresa:

I read a survey my mom did in Ladies Home Journal and she checked off that I've never smoked cigarettes or drank—but I've tried both. I regret it though. I'm a good girl!

Jake:

What I really do on the weekends.

Teresa

Dear Diary,

My dad is soooooo sweet! He just called up to say hi, which is so thoughtful. He knew I had a lotta tests this week.

Of course he asked about my Sweet 16 party plans too. I told him how last week Mom and I went to the store with my brother's ex-girlfriend (we still like her even though they don't go out anymore) and bought all kinds of decorations for my party like candles, cups, tablecloths, plates, forks, streamers, banners, etc. I chose the colors ocean blue, light blue, and white so everything we bought was those colors. It'll be like being underwater. Dad sounds excited to see everything, or at least that's what he said. Of course the party is like 2 weeks away and I told Dad that I am obsessing, as usual. He laughed at me. But that's just me, thinking about stuff all the time. And the more I think about it, the more I think about it!

I know I was saying before that I hate guys, but the truth is there are some good things. Like I do love my dad very much in spite of what I feel about the rest of the male race. My friends have never understood how me and my dad could ever be soooooo close but we are. I was so sad and needy after my parents got divorced. I told Dad I didn't want him to get remarried, not because of my mother, but because of ME!!! I would get SO jealous of his girlfriends. I couldn't help myself. But he is *ALWAYS* here for me.

The only trouble lately with Dad is that I'm growing up. He still sees me as a 6-year-old and not 16! I realize I'm giving him a little more attitude than usual and he clings to me a little bit more and I push him away. But it's not him, it's me. I would do anything for him. Maybe that's why I don't just stay with one guy. I have all the love from a male that I need. Daddy's little girl! Hey, it could be true.

Emma

10/8, 4:03 p.m.

I am in such a bad mood again today and I guess the real reason is that *MY FRIENDS REALLY PISS ME OFF MORE THAN ANYTHING*!!

Today Sherelle and Marybeth are going to the other side of town to see Marybeth's ex-boyfriend. I guess yesterday she asked Sherelle to go with her because she didn't want to go alone. I don't understand why they couldn't have just asked me since they knew I kinda wanted to go. When I said to them, "Oh, you guys are going?" they were like, "Yeah, we're going." I was like "Cool," because whenever we go over there we always do it together, and I just told Marybeth like a week ago that I wanted to see her ex and some of the other guys. What's up with that? And later when I talked to some of the guys on the computer they were like, "Where were you, Em?" And what I feel like saying is, "You know where I was? Left out because my friends don't include me in their plans." I won't get those guys involved though since they'll just go back and tell Sherelle what I said. Then Sherelle would just throw everything back in my face and say I started it. Whatever. Whenever we get in a fight somehow it ends up being my fault.

I think tomorrow when they talk about it in class I will just ignore them. And I'll get over it too because for whatever reason I can't stay mad at either of them.

Marybeth

October 8th

"LOVING SOMEONE FOREVER MEANS LOVING THEM
EVEN IF IT MEANS LETTING THEM LOVE SOMEONE ELSE."

I read that somewhere, I can't remember where. Last night Greg and me broke up for good and I think it was for real. But it was a mutual thing. Right after we broke up though we talked for like another 20 min. and that was great! We were like the best of friends. Today we didn't talk though and I miss him. But this is what I need, I think.

All I've got to say is that love *SUX*! The worst part is that you don't know how much you love someone until it's time to let them go. Like I care so much but it's like what are you gonna do?!! I'm okay not being with him but knowing he is going to be with someone else is what hurts.

I went to a peer ministry meeting tonight. Katie and Em were there too. Also today was the last day of HSPTs and I went car shopping. I think I wanna get a Honda Civic. I saw this dark blue one and I love it! It's 11:45 and I am still so awake. This is not cool.

Emma

10/8, 11:45

I just beeped Adam Marshall twice and he is not calling back. What a jerk! He has to be home because his curfew is 11:30 and who knows what is going on with us. I just beeped him with 911 and he *STILL* didn't call me back. Well, maybe he could be downstairs in his house and forgot his beeper. I really want him to call though. We've been talking every night on AOL and then he calls me and we fall asleep on the phone. No way—the phone is ringing!!

Okay, I'm back and you won't believe this but of all the people in the whole wide world *IT WAS HIM!* I knew it! He's at his friend's house and he couldn't really talk. His friend is so drunk it's funny because he was like yelling at me over the phone. Oh well. Now I can go to bed.

xoxoxoxxoxoxox, emma

Teresa

PAINT BRUSH

I keep my paint brush with me
Wherever I may go,
In case I need to cover up
So the real me doesn't show.
I'm so afraid to show you me,
Afraid of what you'll do—that
You might laugh or say mean things.
I'm afraid I might lose you.

I'd like to remove all my paint coats
To show you the real, true me,
But I want you to try and understand,
I need you to accept what you see.
So if you'll be patient and close your eyes,
I'll strip off my coats real slow.
Please understand how much it hurts
To let the real me show.

Now all my coats are stripped off.
I feel naked, bare, and cold,
And if you still love me with all that you see,
You are my friend, pure as gold.

I need to save my paint brush, though,
And I hold it in my hand,

I want to keep it handy
In case somebody doesn't understand.
So please protect me, my dear friend
And thanks for loving me true,
But please let me keep my paint brush with me
Until I love me, too.

—Bettie B. Youngs

Dear Diary,

I got this from my copy of *Chicken Soup for the Teenage Soul* and I swear by it absolutely. That book is like my bible and I read this poem almost every day. It's all so true. In high school especially, it's so easy to lose your identity just to fit in. I see some people changing just to be in the "in crowd." Why can't people just be themselves? No one is going to like you if you're fake.

Marybeth

October 9th

It's morning now and I'm already late but oh well. I'm wiped out. Last night Greg called me at midnight and we talked until 2:40 a.m. It went well, I think, better than it ever did. He asked me if I wanted to go there, to his house. I said yes but then he made fun of me so I said I wasn't going to. Then he was like nice to me again so I changed my mind. He wouldn't take no for an answer and kept saying, "I'm sorry, please come." But it was too late anyway.

Emma

10/9, 7:35 p.m.

I'm really pissed at Marybeth and Sherelle for ditching me all the time. I dunno but today in school they were being all stupid and it made me think of how they left me at this Sweet 16 last week. I knew they would do it too, which is what sucks the most about all of it. I was having a good time and like dancing all night but then the two of them left to go to a drinking party. I could have gone, but I don't want to get caught. It just bothers me because they are the ones who always get sooooo mad when anyone blows out of a Sweet 16, like it's so rude to do that. Or even worse, when someone totally doesn't even show up. And now here they are doing the same thing. Like no one is going to Amy Greene's party except me and Kevin and Katie, I think. She isn't like really "cool," she's just shy. I really think Sherelle and Marybeth have changed this year. Oh well. I guess I'm over it.

Kevin

Today is Friday and I'm really kind of bored now and I have to go to one of these Sweet 16s again. Everyone is going to all these parties—it gets a little old sometimes. I have to go to this one for Amy Greene. It isn't really gonna be that good because no one will be there—just me, Katie, maybe Em. It should be really really boring. And school today was the worst. I just wanted to go to sleep. I actually think maybe I'll fall asleep before this party.

p.s. Only 10 days left until I drive! Yay!

Katie

October 9
@ 12:54 a.m. (actually Saturday not Friday)
I went to Amy Greene's Sweet 16 party tonight. I felt so bad because not that many people showed up. I mean Amy is the nicest girl—she's just shy! My friends were all invited too, but of course they are too cool to actually go to the party. Em and Kevin were there, but no one else. And that was the *highlight* of my day.

The rest of today was *SO* bad. Where do I start?

I started the day by failing chemistry. I actually think every person in Mr. MacTaggart's class failed,

109

but that didn't matter. It set the mood for the rest of my day. Then I was called to Vice Principal Stern's office and I had a 1-hour meeting with him and Principal Marcus about student events for the year. Okay, that wasn't too bad, but then I got really bad news. We were going over arrangements for Sunday's trip to Red River Theme Park for the Great Fall Rally and I told them one of the Community Club leaders had canceled. They said that wasn't a problem because someone had called and volunteered to be a replacement. To my horror, I was told my ex, Robert, was coming back from college to go. Robert wants to waste a weekend with a bunch of high school kids at an amusement park? What a loser. I hope Brad comes with me so I don't have to worry.

Of course, the day couldn't end on that note. My tennis match was really hideous. We played Webster, which is a pretty good team, and I went in feeling confident that we could beat them. That is . . . until we got there! In the bleachers there were these jerks from Webster and they were harassing me. One guy said, "Nice ass, why don't you take those pants off?" I don't know why it bothered me so much, but it did, and we blew the match because I wasn't concentrating.

I feel bad for Brad because he always has to listen to me complain. I just never want to be the one who messes things up.

Kevin

People are fucked up, including me if I have to be totally honest. I was thinking a lot today about my family for some reason. And yesterday when I said all that about being bored at that Sweet 16. I looked back and saw how pathetic I was being. I shouldn't waste so much time talking like that.

It's funny cuz I was talking to Teresa and she was really upset about something too and I'm thinking what's going on here with all of us is that we can't figure out what we're supposed to be doing or feeling these days. I want Jake to understand this so he can just relax about the whole girl situation. I want Teresa to chill too so she can just calm down and deal with her insecurities and stuff. Everyone is running around trying to be and do everything for everyone else. I keep thinking that someone's gonna wake me up from a dream or something and tell me that a part of my life has been this big ha ha joke's on me.

Okay, so why am I getting all philosophical? I just don't understand so many things about what life is. I am so tired of asking that question. I'm gonna call Adina now.

p.s. Only 9 days left! 9 freakin days until I get my license!

Marybeth

October 10th

I am so so so so so tired! Well, yesterday I was supposed to go see Greg and I never made it there though. He said he was actually a little upset about that. Yeah, it bothered me, but I think in the end it was a good decision. I still have feelings for him. I don't think I can handle just being friends right now. Does that make any sense?

Cross-country track is yucky! Well, it's not bad to run, but three miles around a track at practice can get a little bo-ring! It's 12 laps but it feels like about 50 (good thing we don't do them that often). I've also decided to do basketball again. Last year I blew it off and I missed it so much.

Oh yeah, yesterday that kid Rick Wright wrote me a letter and gave it to me in school. It was actually really cute. He said he likes me a lot and I make him laugh. But he wasn't sure if it was a good time for me, since Greg and me just broke up (sort of). He said he would wait for me if I wanted to be more than friends, but he didn't want to ruin anything because I'm such a good friend to him. And he signed it *Love, Rick*. How sweet is that?

No one has ever done anything like that for me before. I'm not really sure how I should deal with it. I admit that it's a weird situation since I'm still with Greg (sorta). But Rick wants me to tell him how I feel. Could we be more than just friends? I dunno. I just don't want to hurt our friendship. But what should I say? I mean, I still have to figure out what's going on with Greg, right?

I went to this house party tonight but when me and Sherelle got there at 10 it was already breaking up and there was no beer left! After that we went to the Silverado for fries. I came home a little while ago and now it's just midnight, I think. Today I made some extra $$ babysitting so I can put some more money toward the car.

Baxter

October 10

I'm just sitting here on the couch, watching TV. There's some stupid afternoon movie on cable and the actress in it looks a little like Megan. She has the same hair. Lately, I feel like it's so easy for me to fall in love, like with Jessica and now with Megan (I think) but I can't help wonder sometimes why I have never been in a serious relationship before. I don't have a problem with it, but apparently other people do.

I got sick with a cold and cough and fever so I stayed home Thursday and Friday from school and I am still in bed today. *I HATE THAT!* Now I'll have to make up the homework I missed and I bet there is a lot.

Sometimes I wish I could just drop all of these hard classes and take all stupid classes, but I know that life is tough and I can't give up. I also know that in the long run everything will pay off. I really don't want to worry about it.

I have to say though that Billy has totally redeemed himself to me. First he asked how I was feeling when I was out of school. And he didn't call me a wuss like he normally does. Second, he offered to help me with my extra homework. Third, he apologized for not calling me that much lately in general and I thought that was really nice. He told me that he's been really busy with football and work. I'll see what happens, but I think he's really matured since a couple of weeks ago. I'm actually psyched to hang out with him on Sunday at the Red River Community Club rally.

Billy

10-10

Blair D. is getting on my case a little bit. I feel like she follows me around and I know maybe it's because of the age thing, but it's a drag. I don't want her to know what I'm feeling, so I'm not going to call her to do anything this weekend. Just see if she gets the hint. Anyway, I have a lot of other stuff going on. There's the Community Club rally and I have some reading to get done too. I gotta call Baxter now about English. That's about it.

Katie

October 10
@ 9:35 p.m.

Tomorrow we're going to Red River so I have to do lots of stuff. I am determined to have a good time with all the kids from Community Club, even if I do see that *JERK* Robert there.

I was supposed to go to another Sweet 16 tonight but I was really tired so I went to Brad's instead. He had a bunch of people over and they were drinking and having fun. I didn't know his parents weren't going to be there—he didn't tell me. And then they ended up coming home earlier than expected and he got caught. I felt horrible for him, but he betrayed his parents' trust. I felt like saying "I told you so," but he would only get upset and make things worse for both of us.

I follow this strict no drinking policy, which I will *NEVER* break. Drinking is not worth it. Not to me. More and more I find myself around alcohol and it gets easier and easier to resist it and the people around me who are drinking it. I just refuse to even take a single sip. That's it. I tell some jokers that I have this strange and rare blood disease and having alcohol will slant the chemistry in my blood, cause me to seizure, and eventually I will die. Okay, that's a pretty pathetic excuse, I know. But the people I tell it to are dumb enough to believe it and let me alone. Plus, I know more about problems with blood because of my sister Patti's sickness . . . so at least some of what I'm saying has a basis in truth.

I like to do other stuff besides drink. When work gets less busy I'm going to ask Brad to take swing dancing with me. I think it could be fun, but chances are he won't agree. It's the kind of thing I wish we could do to make us closer. I'll see what happens! I know Kevin talked about taking a swing dance class too. Maybe we can all go together.

Later on that same night
@ 11:32

Wow, it's late now and I just got off the phone and I was totally blown away by Brad. He said, "I love you." It just came out of nowhere! I was fighting a little bit with him back and forth and then all of a sudden he just said it to me like he wanted me to just be quiet. It wasn't mumbled or under his breath at all. I don't know how to respond. Should I respond? This has been a weird night. It was all so *unexpected*.

Kevin

10/11

Ok, so I didn't talk to Adina until like 6 tonite and just in the middle of normal conversation I guess I told her that me and Christina had a cool idea that we were gonna sign up for this swing dance class. Then all of a sudden Adina out of nowhere starts in on me like, "I don't trust you" kind of shit. She thinks I'm gonna cheat on her by taking a dance class with Christina (who is just a friend, believe me). So now Adina is like saying that I don't want to be with her. That really makes me frustrated and upset cuz I can't think of what to tell her. What do I say in my own defense?

I really like Adina. So much. We were both pretty upset. Finally we did make up and she realized she was wrong. It's just that she thinks I'm going to do what her last boyfriend did to her, which there is no way I would do. He was a dick, there is no doubt, and he cheated on her bad.

Right now she is at Red River Theme Park with Community Club and the rest of the world and I'm here writing in my diary, so what's really changed? Nothing. We made up but now we're apart again so I don't feel much better. I feel like we're still fighting somehow. Wish I felt better.

p.s. Only 8 more days—yesssss!—until I get my license!

Marybeth

October 11th
So Greg and I talk now but I don't want him back. For now I'm just playing the field . . . you know how

it is. I'm just going to keep doing my own thing. It's cool if me and my BF Sherelle are hanging out with the football players every weekend and go to the parties. I have a blast then, you know? I still have that other football player Rick Wright who likes me, but I dunno. I guess I'm not ready for a relationship or n e thing else. Who knows.

Today I went to Red River to the Community Club rally and it kind of sucked! Well, I had fun, but all those speeches are just so dumb. And I don't feel like hanging around with all these people from Community Club anymore. I thought I would, but it's just so boring having all these stupid meetings. Katie says if I only let it maybe it would change my life, which I think is a cute thing to say but *I DON'T THINK SO!*

At least my girlie Em was there at Red River to make me laugh. Later on we went to hang at the Silverado and I saw Rick W. eating in a booth, only we didn't talk much.

Katie

October 11
@ 10:28 p.m.
Today was a totally ambivalent day! On the one hand, it was awesome and I felt refreshed and renewed, and on the other hand, I felt in great physical pain and confused. Let me start at the beginning . . . Today was

the Community Club Rally at Red River Theme Park. This is a motivational event they set up for Community Club members all over the country, which is a pretty huge group, to get us all in the spirit of service. The rally lasts for like an hour and the rest of the day everyone spends together bonding in the park. We had 60 kids there from JFK.

At 7 a.m. we left the school parking lot crammed into one bus. Half of the kids were still asleep. The rally was unbelievable, but I don't think that many people get much from it because they don't truly open their hearts to the speakers. It got me super motivated, so much so that I climbed onto a row of bleachers and literally fell down four rows. I thought I would keep falling and end up in a hospital somewhere, but this big guy from my homeroom caught me! Still, what a rough way to start the day.

Robert did come home from college to go to the rally. I hadn't seen him in 4 months and was glad to have him out of my life as you can imagine. Well, when I saw him today, I had the weirdest of feelings in my stomach—it was almost as if my heart was crying out at the thoughts of everything that had happened. Abuse, self-criticism, heartache, and self-hate all swirled around me. What I actually thought of most of all surprised me though—which is the betrayal of friends.

When something bad happens to you, you really learn who your friends are. After my year in hell, I could really distinguish true friends from the users.

When Robert and I broke up, I soon found people I considered to be "true" best friends rushing to HIS side and not mine. Like Sherelle, who had been my best friend from kindergarten on. According to her, she decided not to "take sides" because she was "so close to both of us." It made me want to rip my heart out. I think that was definitely the worst moment in my entire life, realizing that people I trusted had betrayed me—and for what? It was the worst feeling in the world.

Anyway, Brad knew all about this and so when he knew Robert would be around, he said he'd come. I was able to pretty much ignore Robert, but I felt a lot better having Brad at my side through it all.

MeanThings MeanThings

Katie:
   I like to treat other people the same
way I expect to be treated—with respect.
Just about the only person I have ever
had mean thoughts about is Rachel Ross and
obviously Robert for all that stuff he
pulled with me last year.

Kevin:
   It's not cool to be mean to
Anyone so I haven't done Anything
major to dis someone except maybe
just like talking back or making fun
a little.

Teresa:
   In 5th grade these other girls and
I made a list of reasons why we
hated this one girl in our class
named Nicole. Then we gave her the list.

Billy:
   I thought it was no big deal but in third grade
I told my best friend's secret. He's still
embarrassed and he still won't talk to me.

MeanThings MeanThings

Marybeth:

I'm such a BIG wiseass and sometimes I think that maybe I take my jokes too far.

Jake:

If me and Kevin don't like someone we can both be assholes to piss them off and we team up to do it.

Emma:

When I was 6, I spit in my mom's face and she got really mad at me. Sometimes I just get really mad about stuff and I guess I always have.

Baxter:

Usually it's me who gets picked on and not the other way around.

Emma

Yesterday I went to Red River with Community Club. It was so much fun. I ran into this kid Sam from the other high school in town—Joyce. I hadn't seen him in something like 2 months, and when I saw him I was so excited. Well, he was there with this kid named Adam Fitzhugh (that's a cool last name) who's really cute! And it turns out that he wants to hook up with me!

Well, me and Adam F. didn't really hook up yesterday, but he kissed me a couple of times. But wait! This isn't a good thing, see, I have a *HUGE* problem. There's the other Adam who I've been seeing and talking to. Adam Marshall. And he's really cool and all too!

I'm just not ready to settle down with one person. I dunno.

WHAT AM I GONNA DO?

Today when I got home from shopping I got an e-mail from Adam M. He said all this stuff about how he will wait for me to be ready to have a relationship no matter how long it takes and that he really likes me. I wrote him back to say that I do like talking to him but that I'm not ready to settle down just yet. I hope I didn't hurt his feelings but I had to tell him the truth.

I hate dealing with stuff like this. I seriously

thought I was going to cry when I came home. I just get really stressed when it comes to this stuff. I dunno.

I JUST WANT TO BE ABLE TO DO WHAT I WANT AND HOOK UP WITH WHOEVER I WANT.

I hope things work out for the best.

I just went offline and Adam F., the Adam I met today, is gonna call me at 10:30. I'm kinda excited about that. I'll write more about him 2morrow. The good thing is that Kevin's party is coming up too so maybe someone will be able to go to the party with me or I'll see them there.

Kevin

10/12

Ohh man, today was a decent day. So I can just say that I don't really understand my chemistry class at all. It's really hard stuff. Actually it isn't hard—it's just not taught right. Why did I have to get stuck with this teacher? I'm really stressed out right now because I have a bunch of things to do for my party and I have to do it before Thursday and if I don't get them done I'm gonna be screwed! On top of all that I have to memorize 83 ions. Wahoo! That's a lot of fun. Then I have to make a pretty big report for my Spanish class and also an algebra test. So I gotta go study *NOW.* Jake's gonna come over too. Ta ta, Kevin p.s. We got our class rings today

p.p.s. Only 7 more days until I get my license!

p.p.p.s. Only 5 more days until my party—yessssss!

Jake

October 12

In only 5 *DAYS* Kevin's having his birthday party, which I think should be awesome. He invited something like 160 people and I really think everyone is going to be there. All of them are my closest friends too like Lazlo and Micky, DJ Jonny, May, and other girls like Teresa and Marybeth too. Kevin said he even asked Billy and some of the other guys from the football team. It's a cool party with a DJ (this guy Scott who's actually leaving for California after the party is over). Our parents are coming too, which is okay because it's not a drinking party or anything. Of course my dad won't be there, but my mom will. I can't wait to go because I love to dance and I know all the ladies will be dancing with me because I'm looking pretty good these days. Oh yeah, and today I got my class ring, which looks good too.

Baxter

October 12

The beginning part of today before lunch was really awesome because I hung out with Jessica and her best friend Megan. I like her SO much. I showed them my new class ring. It was so cool.

The later part of today sucked. Miss Shapiro, the evil tyrant that runs Community Club, said that I stink as the public relations person for the group. She said I didn't do enough at Red River. In front of everyone she humiliated and degraded me. I hate her. That stupid rally was not that important anyway.

Emma

10/13, 8:39 p.m.

Yesterday at school we got our class rings. I'm looking at mine right now. It's gold with a little blue stone in the middle. One side has my name and the other side says Bulldogs with the year 2000 on it. The 2000 is written really cool.

I don't feel that well. My throat and ears hurt and my voice has been disappearing. I'm curled up in a ball on my bed watching my soap opera and I'm really confused! What is going on? I haven't seen it in a while.

Last night I was on the phone until 1:00 a.m. talking to Adam F. It was a *really* good conversation. Most of what we talked about was the other Adam, Adam M. They go to the same school and they're actually friends, if you can believe it.

But when Adam M. e-mailed me to say how he felt, that made me feel strange. And I was telling this to Adam F. on the phone and he was like, "Do you like Adam Marshall or what?" and I said, "Yeah, I guess," but I'm not ready for a relationship. I don't think that's what he wanted to hear.

Well, later that night I was online with Adam M. and he gave me *such* attitude! I was so pissed. I think maybe they had talked to each other and Adam F. told Adam M. what I had said. Whatever. If Adam M. can't deal with my liking Adam F. too, then too bad for him, right? He can just screw off.

God, I really hope that Adam M. doesn't make a big deal out of this to Adam F. because I feel really bad about it. Like I didn't plan for all this to happen—it just did. I wish Adam F. would call me again right now. I don't know whether to keep talking to Adam M. or not. I'll decide when Adam F. calls.

What am I going to wear to Kevin's party this weekend? I need to look awesome because Scott the DJ is going to be there. I want to wear something Scott will like since it's the last party he's going to DJ at before moving to California. He's a great guy and I'm going to miss him so much.

Katie

Everyone is starting to talk about Kevin's birthday party and I'm sad I won't be there. I have to go away on a weekend church retreat. But I know that I am making the right choice. The retreat is what I need to do.

I've been feeling so sentimental lately (like getting emotional at the rally and all). It's just that when I know I'm going to miss a major event like Kevin's birthday, I can't help but think about each of my friends. Ever since grammar school we were this very tightly knit group, but I guess we don't really hang out together that much anymore. For me this group was Marybeth, Emma, Kevin, Jake, Baxter (Teresa after freshman year), and sometimes Billy and we would do everything together as freshmen and sometimes sophomores, but now we're split up. Kevin's party would have been cool because everyone will be together.

My chem tutor came today and he was as confused as me about the work I was doing, which was so weird. Isn't he supposed to know what he's doing? Well, it ended up making me feel better knowing that he *didn't* know everything. I hate the fact that I am trying so hard and I am not getting the results I want so badly. I suppose I will survive. There are moments like today when I realize that I can't do it all, but I just can't slow down either. Good thing I have no tennis practice or match today because I am feeling a little burned out by that too.

Emma

10/14, too early

I really am sick. I didn't go to school today. It's too early (well, actually 8:10 a.m.) and I should roll over and sleep to get better but I can't sleep. This always happens when I'm sick—I become an insomniac for some reason when most of my friends just get stoned on cold medicine. Oh well. Anyway, I really hate being sick and missing school. Is that strange?

I have a really important math quiz tomorrow so I'll have to go to school. Oh—and I have to get ready for Kevin's big party over the weekend. I won't be sick for that!

The biggest news today is that Adam M. was not mad at Adam F. for talking to me about him and I was getting all upset for nothing! And thank God for that too because really Adam F. didn't do anything wrong. But now Adam M. says he isn't interested in me anymore. That bothers me because I don't think it's fair to me. I can't help what I feel.

And online just now Adam M. was saying how he's gonna go back to drinking and smoking and that really worries me because his friend died two months ago because of drunk driving. What if the same thing happened to Adam M.? Adam F. says Adam M. is making the whole thing up to make me feel guilty, so I'll see and talk to him more. What am I supposed to believe? I'm confused.

10/14, later on that day

I'm feeling a lot better now. I took more of that cherry medicine. When I went online after dinner Adam M. came on with this big long letter about how sorry he was. Can you believe that? I swear Adam F. had something to do with it. And I accepted Adam M.'s apology, of course. Hey, at least he still wants to talk, which is a good sign, right? Even if I don't want to hook up with him I can't have him being mad at me.

Ahhhh! I am so pissed because I just realized we have no more tissues and my nose is running and I need some. Dad said we ran out this morning, so did he buy some? Of course not. I hate being sick—it's a pain in the ass. The only good part is being in my room. I have those glow-in-the-dark stars on my ceiling and when I'm in here alone I turn off the lights and there's this eerie glow. I like it that way. When I'm in here I don't have to listen to my parents yelling either. Well, I'm feeling a lot worse so I'm gonna try and sleep some more.

Katie

Another late night. I suppose I will just have to run on (adrenaline) tomorrow. I didn't get home from my tennis match until 7:30 and then I had math tutoring until 8:30. I had to watch Dawson's Creek, which I taped, so I did that and studied for 2 tests that I have tomorrow. I talked with Brad briefly, but nothing much.

What a fiasco at tennis today with Rachel Ross! That stupid $%&@! Why can't she just mind her own business? She was running all over the court and she couldn't get one lob back in play to save her life. Her opponent in the game was so sick of her cheating that she was screaming up and down. It was embarrassing, that's for sure. I don't think she even begins to realize what a fool she is.

The worst part about Rachel sometimes is that she is oblivious to what she's doing. And that makes me angrier than anything else. You can't just walk through life blind to what you're doing and saying that may be hurting other people's feelings. I consider myself to be pretty aware of this stuff. Rachel thinks she is so smart. I just hate her so much.

On Dawson's Creek tonight, when Dawson and Joey almost had a fight, I was thinking again about how much that show is like my real life. I almost can't

131

wait until Brad and I have our first fight. I think that when people make up it always brings the relationship closer.

Teresa

Oct 14

Dear Diary,

Okay. I watch the show Dawson's Creek, but it makes me kind of mad at the same time. Everyone's so perfect and beautiful and they all run around with each other in this perfect place. I mean the guys on the show are cute, but it is not exactly a page from MY life.

I have this thing against groups of friends like that. Cliques are too exclusive and someone just always gets hurt. It's just wrong and unfair. I am sooooo opinionated on the subject—just ask Kevin. I can't even count the number of times I've cried on his shoulder about feeling left out. I even wrote a poem about how I feel.

FOLLOWING CIRCLES

They stand in an exclusive group,
Excluding themselves from the rest
Talking, laughing, and snapping gum,
Thinking they are better than the rest.

Guys, money, and popularity
Are the sacraments of this crowd
Nothing and no one else matters
They are obnoxious and loud.

Guys are the only thing that matters,
And of course they do drugs and drink
They are shallow and insincere
And unless they're together, they can't think.

They walk around like snobs,
Gossip and strut their stuff,
They ignore anyone who's not like them
And think they're the ones who are tough.

But they are really the lonely ones
Who will end up without anyone
Was it really worth all that superiority
Just for a few years worth of fun?

Don't get caught up in a clique
You will just end up a petty fool
Maybe you think you're in the right circles
But the truth is it's very uncool.

Baxter

WHAT IS EVERYBODY'S PROBLEM?

I don't understand—why is everyone so afraid of being left out? I'm left out of things all the time and I'm ok. Like Emma is always saying how pissed she is because of Marybeth and Sherelle always going out and how they have all these "in" jokes and she feels so out of it. What's that about?

Today I had a really hard physics test. I think I did ok though. Tomorrow I have a math analysis quiz. I'm a little confused but my teacher is never there after school so I guess extra help is out of the question. But I'm not going to worry. I don't get as upset as Katie does when she can't do her math problems. She gets really worked up, which I don't understand at all.

And why do so many people hate their parents? Everyone acts like it's a chore to do stuff with their families, but not me. I was talking to Billy today and he was stressed out about his dad. He has this whole thing about doing well to please his family, but the truth is I don't think they put that much pressure on him. I think Billy should just relax.

Billy

10-15

I've been so busy and I feel crazy. I'm supposed to be finished with this one book for English and I'm not finished. My dad is going to be really disappointed if I don't do well in that class, so I better read. I'm always so busy with school and sports that sometimes it's hard to know what to do first. My brother Lee says everything is what you make of it, whatever that means.

I actually had a good time last week at the Community Club rally at Red River. I think I made a really good friend—Keith. He was my friend before but we sort of bonded again and it was pretty cool.

Another cool thing that happened was that I just picked up our new car and it's a used Mazda with only 20,000 miles. It's silver and it has a sunroof and it is so fine. We're putting awesome speakers in the back *and* it has leather seats. I love it. Well, GTG for now.

Baxter

October 16

A lot of things pissed me off today.

First of all there was another stupid test we had to take. I am so *sick of these tests*! Enough already. The stupid state wants to make the HSPT harder than it is so they gave us a field test to see how we would do. Everyone knew the test didn't count so half the kids left the test blank and just walked out. I gave some half-ass answers and wrote a note to the testing people. I wrote that I felt these tests were a complete waste of time and that they shouldn't treat us like guinea pigs.

I also found out today that Katie told her entire tennis team that I had a crush on Jessica. *I could die!* First of all she should have never said *ANYTHING* to anyone! I trusted her and boy, was that stupid. Besides, I like Megan now and not Jessica.

It just got me so upset. I don't want to make any waves with Katie, but she has to understand that I have feelings too and she just can't be trusted. I knew she'd been talking to people like Em about it, and that didn't bother me as much, although it did bother me. She just has no right to do this to me or anyone else. I think the person I least trust is her, definitely. I always thought I could and I don't hate her for it— I'm just embarrassed. She always blows stuff way out of proportion. It's really not a big deal.

The reason I'm writing in my diary right now and not out with any of my friends even though it's Friday night is because I called Kevin and Jake to do something and they never called me back. They probably went out and never bothered to ask me. So once again I'm ditched. I'm really sick and tired of them never including me in what they do. Then again maybe Kevin is just getting ready for his party and he's too busy. I hope that's what it is.

Is there something wrong with me? Why does everything seem to be going *wrong*?

I'm crossing my fingers that Kevin's party will be a really fun time since everyone is going to be there. I hope I see Megan. That would be perfect.

Katie

October 16
@ 9:50 p.m.

Well, today was a *PERFECT* day for me. I am away on this retreat. It is the best! I had a good day in school too (I am averaging an A+ in AP history). Then I had a Community Club meeting and tennis. Around 6:15 I went over to the church to get ready for the retreat and we left at 7 or so. Brad came to say goodbye to me. All the other peer ministers are so cool. Everyone is in this together and we are really bonding! I had to do a talk tonight in front of everyone—basically a 10-minute shpeel on who I am and what my life has been about + a song. I did a taking risks talk and told everyone about a little boy who I befriended at the hospital when I was visiting my sister. I think I made a real impact. Tomorrow there will be more talks and activities. It should be really good.

The place where we're staying is so beautiful too. It has to be one of the most peaceful places around here, and there is nothing within 50 miles except trees! My only regret is that I can't wish Kevin a happy birthday in person.

Billy

I'm psyched because Kevin is having his party tomorrow and I'm going to bring Blair D. She's really into it. It seems like I'm so stretched out lately. Football at 7:00 and then homework doesn't get done until like 11 at night.

I was thinking about last weekend's Community Club Red River trip again. I guess I was being sort of obvious scoping out this other girl Grace who was there. The bad part is that she's Blair's good friend. Yeah, that could be a very bad thing. The thing is that Blair D. is the one who likes me, so I have to stop checking out other girls. I feel like *all I have been doing for the past few days is having women worries*!!

And it gets more complicated too because somehow after the rally Grace found out that I liked her, or at least that I thought she was hot. I think one of the guys on the team told her and then she spilled the beans to Blair D.

To tell you the truth, it won't be a problem for very long because I think it's getting serious between Blair D. and me. And she'll forgive me. Still, I can't just all of a sudden stop liking Grace. She is really a hottie. I guess I'm causing trouble here. I should just be happy that I have any g/f *at all* right now.

So Blair D. told me she's wearing this really hot outfit to Kevin's party tomorrow, and I can't wait to see. If I have an idea about the perfect girl, is it wrong to ask for that in someone else when I'm not perfect myself? I'm just gonna see what happens. Maybe Grace will show up too.

Kevin

10/16

Ohhh man, now today is *REALLY REALLY* good and I'm in a much better mood than I have been. Ok, well, to start today off right we took another *stupid* test in school that was soooo pointless—but I dealt with it. Then I found out that I got a B+ on that math test I took on Wed. The Spanish report went really well too and I had fun, believe it or not. Then I had a real kick ass time in gym today. We played tennis and of course I sucked, but we were having some real fun just messing around. I wish I had more classes with my friend Christina—she is like my soul sister, we are sooo freakin great and fun together. Ok, besides that, when I got to chem class the teacher said we would postpone the test by a day so now it will be next

Tuesday, which is *very* good news. And finally he explained how to do all the work I have been completely lost on. That was awesome. I get it now—finally!

After school was just as good too. When I got home I got all this candy from Price Club for my party tomorrow. Part of me hopes we don't use it all so I can get leftovers . . . heeheehee. Um, then my neighbor helped me put the wing on my car and it looks really phat, I know it. Then he told me he would paint it a week from Saturday. In two Saturdays my car will be done and I am so happy about that.

Then me, Adina, and Lazlo went to the mall and I got Adina an anniversary present (yesterday it was one whole month!). It's this really really cute giraffe doll cuz she loves big animals like giraffes, lions, zebras (and me!). Anyway, I got that and I got a necklace too and put my class ring on it for her. I'm going to put it around the giraffe's neck with a note telling her how I feel about her. I sooo love her. She is making me sooo happy and I haven't felt like this in a while. Then I got this phat black shiny shirt for my party. I can't wait until tomorrow. It will be such a kick ass party—I am gonna love it sooo much.

p.s. *I GET MY LICENSE IN ONLY 3 DAYS!!!!*

This is the most awesome thing that has ever happened to me in my entire life.

Teresa

Dear Diary,

Even though I say it doesn't matter I'm still looking for love! I keep thinking about Kevin's party and
how I want to look good and I know that is just
STUPID. I guess I do still want something from my
relationship with him. I just can't let go.

For some reason I'm the only one out of my
friends who has not been in some kind of a long-term
relationship. I get scared because is it my fault? What
am I doing wrong?

I had such a great horoscope the other day about
love and social life. Sometimes I believe in these
but sometimes I swear it's like the *OPPOSITE*
of reality:

**Meeting guys is easy all month thanks to your
party schedule. You might even be doing
some boy chasing, not very Libra-like, but
lots of fun. You're daydreaming about a cur-
rent crush and former flame—and at parties,
girls stay close to you to meet new guys. And
watch out! You're a total guy magnet on the
9th, 17th, and 24th.**

Billy

I don't know how serious Blair D. and me are gonna get, or if this is a more permanent kind of arrangement or what. I mean, sex is a big deal and there are so many rules to it. But I'm not saying I don't want it, because I do.

Right now Blair D. is more than just a hookup, it's true. There is definitely more there than just a kiss. There's a really special connection between us. That's why I think hookups are bullshit because nothing can come of it but trouble. The girl suddenly thinks you're together and then her friends all call you and harass you about it. It's crazy. But sex is really serious and when Blair and I decide to do it, it will be serious. She says she thinks she'll be ready in 6 months. I hope it will be sooner, but I'll give her the time—that's the right thing to do.

What About Sex?   What About Sex?

Marybeth:

I don't know what I think anymore about sex. Last spring this guy I was seeing was a little pushy about the whole sex thing. I mean, we didn't do anything, like he didn't force me, but things got kinda mixed up in my head. It didn't feel right.

I mean, I don't believe in chastity or anything, but I do think you need to be in love before sex.

Billy:

I'm definitely needy for sex and plenty of it! What guy isn't? Ha ha! In all seriousness though since I'm already 17, I really feel I'm mature enough to handle that kind of situation. People always talk about sex being with the right person and I think that is so true. It's just that most people have problems figuring out who the "right" person is, right? In my case, Blair D. is clean and has a great personality and that's "right" for me, but I know some other people have other definitions of what is "right." I think

about 95% of JFK would have sex today if
they had the right person. A lot of the guys
on the team have so many one night hookups
and the stories I hear are crazy. It's kind of
hard to respect that.

Katie:

I know a lot of people think it's okay
for teenagers to have sex if they really
love someone, but I disagree. The teenage
years are full of constant confusion,
uncertainty, and feelings of depression, and a
teenager is in no way ready to decide if
they really, truly love a person or to
deal with the baggage that comes with sex.
I've hooked up with a few people in the
past year, but it really doesn't go very
far. I had some problems dealing with this
when I was with Robert, but I am happy
now because Brad respects my decisions.

Baxter:

Now, every guy in his right mind wants sex, but that's
not really what I'm looking for. I just don't think

people should be sleeping with everybody else. And not only because sex diseases can literally kill you. People need to have feelings for each other before they have sex. That way they know what they are getting into, pardon the pun.

Teresa:

Guys are always out for one thing as far as I can tell. Sometimes I wonder, is sex all they think about? The answer is mostly YES! I may only be turning 16, but I have been through soooo much already. (It's not how many birthdays you have — it's how many experiences you've had.) I know I'm much more mature than most kids my age. You can never give in sexually to a guy until you know he's for real.

Kevin:

YEAh, sex! BRing it on now! J/K, hA hA! No, but seRiously I'll wAit foR sex until I know it's ReAlly love And we ARe both ReAdy. Now,

AdinA hAS SAid she isn't reAdy And won't be foR A while And I pretty much feel the sAme wAy. I wAnt it to be greAt And if she is the one I'm cool with wAiting foR her cuz she is soooo worth it.

Emma:

Sex. What a scary and important word. I'm nowhere near ready to have sex. There are so many risks involved. Getting pregnant and getting STDs are the two main worries that I have. I want to wait till I'm married, but I'm not sure that will happen. If the guy I was with wanted to have sex, I would just tell him straight up that I wasn't ready. No one's ever broken up with me because of that.

Jake:

I want to have sex but not with just anyone. It has to be just right, especially the first time. I have to love the girl and I'm not going to do it while she or I am drunk or just in my car. It will be after dinner and dessert, in a bed with music and definitely plenty of protection. I do dream about hardcore sex with some girls when I want to jerk off or whatever, but that will come way down the road after I've experienced real love and romance.

Marybeth

October 17th

I'm at a total loss as far as this Greg thing goes. I don't know if I'm so clear on the Rick Wright thing either. I just want to do the right thing for everyone involved. I don't know if that means sex or what.

People have been annoying me pretty easily lately. I don't know why. Maybe because they keep saying stupid stuff about me. I mean, I've gone out with so many different guys and I bet that if you took a poll more than 95 percent of them would have no idea what romance is. But this guy Rick does and that has me a little bit confused. Greg was just a summer thing, and we're broken up now, but we're still like friends with benefits and I like the way that's working out 4 me.

I JUST NEED TRUST!

If anything at all is going to happen between me and one of these guys I need to trust him. I know this from experience. Last year I hooked up with this one guy out of pity (I know it sounds wrong 2 do, but that's what it was). Then he told all his friends that I blew him! And that was not cool. He's the one who *SUX!* So now I don't really trust anyone and I definitely won't do anything unless I know the guy a little.

Kevin's party is tonite and I'm not going 2 let all this bring me down. I'm going 2 have fun!!

Baxter

October 17

I am really depressed that Megan hasn't called back. I really like her and she's not giving me any straight signals. She flirts with me in school but then she never calls me back. Last night I even lost sleep because I was worrying about her not calling me.

I know I'm the last person in the world who should think he has a hope with someone like her, but I do. I don't know shit about relationships, but I don't want pity. I just keep trying. I think maybe it's just really a bad thing that I wear my heart on my sleeve, you know? I've fallen "in love" a lot of times, like everyone else I know, but it doesn't mean I've ever been loved in return. And for whatever reason the girls that I like apparently have a problem with the fact that I haven't really been with anyone. They want some guy who's experienced, I guess.

Maybe Kevin's party will take my mind off this. I'm getting a headache.

Emma

10/17, 6:12 p.m.

I just got back from the football game and my head is pounding. We won and my friends played so good but it was sooooo loud there! My friend got 5 touchdowns, which is like unbelievable! Adam F. came to the game too. He is so cute. I dunno. Adam M. wants to take me to the movies next Friday and I told him I maybe have to babysit. Marybeth and Sherelle say I should just go and hang out or whatever and not get so stressed about what's the right thing to do. But I really don't want to go. I don't want anyone to think that I want a relationship with either of them. I dunno—maybe I just have to say from the beginning that we're friends and that's it.

I'm waiting for my dad to come home with my dinner and I'm absolutely starving right now. Then I have to take a shower and get ready for Kevin's party. I know I'm going to be so upset after the party because Scott the DJ is moving back to California. Actually Scott's a dancer too (not just a DJ) and I've known him ever since I was twelve. Every party he does, me and him ALWAYS dance. He just turned 20, and I know he's a lot older than me, but we always have so much fun dancing together! I'm going to miss him like so much.

Kevin

10/18
Ok, I am totally nervous as shit. I can't take it any longer at all. I just have to relax and not think about

it or I'm gonna get all fidgety all over again. My party was last night. I was having a whole shitload of fun until the middle of the night. Then this guy Jon showed up when he was NOT invited. He used to go out with Jake's ex-woman Claudia. Well, he showed up shitfaced and so we asked him nicely to leave (me and Jake and our friends Micky and Mick). But Jon was being a total dick. We got really pissed and then he was all up in Mick Lazlo's face trying to start shit with him. Then he wouldn't leave and I told my 'rents and the dancer, this guy Scott who's got arms like my thighs, I swear. He's moving to California soon and he doesn't really give a shit about Jon so he told him he better leave or else he'd make him leave. But I couldn't believe it—this jerk still was trying to start shit. Well, he went outside and a big fight broke out. All in all he made my dad have to call the cops 2X. I don't know what's going on but quite frankly I hope he dies a violent death. Well, I don't mean that, but I do. And I'm not even a violent person. I did try to have fun after that but it kind of ruined some stuff and it was my party, which REALLY sucked.

p.s. Tomorrow I turn 17 for real!!!!—*ONE MORE DAY AND I GET MY LICENSE. YESSSSSS!*

Jake

Hey! Well Kevin's party was awesome. I had such a good time and I know he did too. I brought some girl with me from Joyce. We hang with kids from there sometimes and she is really hot and can dance good too. Still there is just something I don't like about her and I don't know what it is, it's weird. So I don't want to date her or anything, I just thought she'd be a fun party date. The only bad thing at the party was this hardass Jon Barry. He came uninvited and picked fights with everyone there because he was drunk off his ass and we told him to get the hell out. He thinks he is the toughest kid in the school but he is so wrong. He is just one big mole—that is what he looks like. I especially don't like him because he is the jerk who messed with Claudia's head. He hated me when I was going out with her and he still kept trying to go out with her. He was being such an asshole to Mick Lazlo. He will never be mature no matter what, he just doesn't get it. I don't know if he has any real friends or what. The bad thing is that I think Claudia is seeing more of him again. She said she needed more time to think about us, but all she wanted to do was run back to that jerk. Tonight she even left for a while after he crashed the party. She went to go talk to him. What a joke.

Truthfully, she has become more of a bitch lately and I can't really stand to be around her anymore. It just is not the same as it used to be. I'm just looking for a nice girl who is pretty and has a good body and will treat me good. So far I haven't found any.

Teresa

Dear Diary,

Kevin's party was *AWESOME*! But my horoscope was *wrong* and I didn't meet any cute guys *at all*. Plus my hair looked bad for some reason—it was too curly. And I think I looked kind of fat. Everyone else looked *great*!

I thought maybe this guy Andy I've been flirting with would show up but he and Kevin don't really get along so I guess he wasn't even invited. Kevin and Jake and Jonny danced with me, of course, but I think they were just doing it to be nice. When I came home I wrote this poem. I don't know why I was feeling so intense—I just was. I guess that's why I love poetry so much. I don't have to show it to anyone, I don't have to talk to anyone, and I can express everything I'm feeling. I can be and say whatever I want and no one can stop me.

UNDERNEATH

My heart is hurting
it is in so much pain
For many reasons,
I feel like I'm going insane.

How can I be treated
this terrible way?
Why do I feel
Like I am not okay?

This is not the only time
I have felt alienation
It is like this every day,
I always have this sensation.

Sometimes I want to stop it,
And I think I can
But then it creeps up on me
And it gets out of hand.

There is no worse feeling
Than feeling no way out.
When you need to feel needed
But all you have is doubt

Is there one single person
that loves me out there?

Is there one single person
to REALLY show they care?

Sometimes I spend time thinking
How it's all an awful game,
that no one REALLY cares,
that everyone is the same.

Is there one person out there
to rescue me from this sadness?
Is there a person out there
who can take me away from my madness?

I want everyone to know
the open person I can be.
There is so much really there,
beneath what they see.

I want someone to take me
Out of my own private hell
I want someone to see me
See what lies underneath my shell.

One Thing My Friends

Jake:
How much pain I go through every day with my dad.

Teresa:
I get angry with them ~~because~~ they're so into their stupid little groups and always have to do everything together. That's why I don't choose to hang out with them sometimes. I refuse to ~~be~~ part of some clique.

Billy:
My friends don't know what a sensitive guy I am. I come across as a big football player, but I'm actually sweet and sensitive.

Katie:
My friends know basically everything. The only thing is that they don't think about too far in the future vs. the way I think. I am planning things out way in advance, and sometimes I don't think my friends understand what it feels like to have serious goals like mine.

Don't KnowAboutMe

Marybeth:

Sometimes I get kinda depressed. I mean, I usually feel ok pretty quick, but in the past I've thought about some pretty serious stuff. I think we all have.

Baxter:

I laugh along with them and try not to be bothered, but I really hate it when they make fun of me.

Emma:

I feel lonely because my friends don't want me, like maybe I'm not good enough for them.

Kevin:

My friends don't have the slightest idea how much I really miss my sister Lena or how much I cry over that time in my life—but I think that's just cuz they're afraid to ask me about it for fear of my pain.

Marybeth

October 18th

Well, it's Sunday and I'm exhausted. Yesterday I went to Kevin's party and it was fun! Also yesterday I went to the school's football game and we won! Today I went to the boys' soccer game. It was a county game and we won in overtime. Our teams are doing pretty good this year so far. After that, Emma, Rick Wright, and I went to the mall. It was pretty boring. So then we came back to my house and had dinner and that was cool.

Oh, I am so ecstatic! I bought a car and I pick it up tomorrow. It sucks though because it completely cleaned out my savings account and I have been saving for like my *WHOLE LIFE,* literally. Now I have to save $$ for insurance. These days I am living on a budget but it's worth it.

I feel really bad 4 Em lately. She's really upset over a whole bunch of things (like Adam F., Adam M., and Scott going to California).

Emma

10/18, 10:00 a.m.

It's morning but I can't sleep anymore. Every time I close my eyes I see Scott. Last night at Kevin's party was horrible. When I walked in at first I was ok but then after an hour or so I started to get all knotted up inside. I guess I didn't realize how much I liked him. He came up to me and said I was his favorite and that I should never forget that. Then me and him danced the last dance of the party and all I did the whole time was cry on his shoulder. He just was holding me and I think he almost started to cry too. I know he wanted to. It was so awful. He remembered my e-mail screen name and absolutely promised to get in touch as soon as he got to California next week. I have to stop talking about this because just writing it all down is making me sad all over again.

And now I have to go to Katie's house for a *STUPID* Community Club meeting that's supposed to last for 4 hours! I can't believe it. Baxter and I both think it's a drag. And I agree with him that Miss Shapiro is being so nasty lately. Of course she isn't the same way to Katie, but whatever. It's just that's the last place I want to be right now, but it's a mandatory meeting so I'll have to go. I'm just not in the mood to listen to Miss Shapiro lecture us on all the things we do wrong. I mean, we all started out in the club because we wanted to have some fun and we do good stuff, but then she has to criticize us and ruin it. Whatever. All I know is that Baxter and I and a *LOT* of other people just don't want to be a part of it anymore. I think maybe we should tell Katie the truth.

October 19

Boy, do I have a lot to talk about. First of all, I finally told Katie that I didn't like how she told the entire tennis team I had a crush on Jessica. She told me she was really sorry and she wouldn't bring it up again. She's a good friend, I guess, I just wish the whole thing hadn't gotten so messed up.

Saturday night was Kevin's party and it was great! There was nothing but great music and great dancing. Everybody was all over me 'cause I'm a stud.

Oh—and Kevin passed his official driving test today so he's gonna be cruising around now, which is one of the coolest things that's happened in a long time.

Now, the *BIG* news! Today at school I was taking pictures at Megan's table (I had one of those instant cameras as a goof) and without me even asking her she gave me her beeper #. Here's the note:

Megan's beeper
555-0023 and punch in 68

So tonight I called the number and we talked for about half an hour. And there was a lot of flirtation going on. She was calling me dumb and I was calling her idiot and there was that lovely *FIRE!! Boy, do I love her.* She is sweet, cute, funny, and perfect. Hopefully we will be going out soon. I think she might be it!

Katie

October 19
@ 12:30 a.m.

Wow, what a weekend. I am home from the retreat and it's this incredible stress-free feeling I can't really even describe. A happy form of contentedness like nothing else. I really think that my talk, which was one of the first ones of the weekend, did a lot to inspire everyone for the rest of the time. I dedicated it to my family, especially Patti, who is feeling sick again these days.

Saturday it was great and terrible at the same time. On the retreat, everyone talked about a topic like friends or family and it got pretty emotional. This one kid was talking about how his father died *while* their parents were getting a divorce, and then even worse, this other kid talked about her mom's death and how it taught her to live for today more. About halfway through she broke down, and then we all broke down too, and everyone was crying.

So here I am now on the bus ride back and we're playing some stupid game. This retreat team is really unbelievable. I hope we can all stay close.

p.s. I almost forgot that I called Kevin yesterday to wish him luck at the party. He sounded so happy. I wish I could have gone, but oh well.

Marybeth

October 19th

Kevin got his license! I am sooooo happy for him. Today he called all of us and told us that he was going to take out his wheels. Ha! It's a great day 4 me too since I picked up my Civic and it looks great. I love it so much and now all I need is my license, right? That sucks!!!! But my mom gave me this funny bumper sticker.

```
Clear the Road—I'm SIXTEEN!
```

I was just on the phone with Rick Wright. Now I'm on the phone with Sherelle. She says that Wright wants her to hook us up. I don't know about that one. Though I do want to start talking to a guy or hooking up with someone. Gotta go to some more parties, I guess. Tomorrow are the dreaded PSATs—*NOT* a party.

Emma

10/20, 9:27 p.m.

Kevin got his license, which is so awesome! Now we have someone to drive us places. Just kidding. He spends all his time with Adina anyhow.

It's been a couple of days and no, Scott has not e-mailed me from California yet. Next week is Teresa's Sweet 16 and it's gonna be the 1st party that Scott is not going to be at. I'll probably get all upset again. I don't know why. I only ever saw him at parties where he was working, but I guess I've just had a crush on him for so long and he's always been around. I will just keep going online to see if he has written.

xoxoxoxox (to Scott!)

Katie

October 21
@ 5 p.m.

I am crying on my bathroom floor right now . . . it feels so awful. I don't know why I am so upset but I just need to cry. My tennis coach yelled at us today and I also did badly in chem again. It feels really bad to try so hard and not find success. I just need to cry.

Why does everything have to be so hard? My mom

is comparing my problems to other kids' problems and trying to fix my life for me. I don't want or need someone to fix everything or tell me what I do wrong. I only want someone to listen to me and just care about me. I don't need to be pushed—I do enough of that myself. "You're just not trying hard enough!" she says. But I am. I am! I am trying *so hard* but it just doesn't show. I'm so fed up and frustrated with life. Plus I look horrible right now. I have to do something because later on there's an important Community Club meeting over here. Suck it up, Katie.

Marybeth

October 21st

Well, yesterday I got my hair cut short but I like it because it's curly. It usually never gets curly but for some reason it works like this.

I had an English quiz today and pretty much failed it, which is awful but for some reason I just do not care about that stuff. Mr. Sonstein is such a schmuck too. I saw him in the corridor at school and he said, "Miss Miller, you have been doing very well so far." I said thanks and after that he went on to say how bad everyone else is doing while I stay afloat, and I should be very proud of my accomplishments. I guess that was a nice thing for me to hear, but I still think he's a shmuck.

You know what I *REALLY* want? I want one of those Teen magazine makeovers. I've always wondered how someone gets picked for those because I've written ever since I was 13 and no one ever sent me any reply. Oh well, what am I complaining about? I have a Community Club meeting in like 10 minutes. Gotta go.

Emma

10/21, 5:55 p.m.

I want to write more about my friend Cliff. I haven't really talked about him much, but that just may be changing. Cliff and I went to kindergarten together and then he went away to another school. Then like 2 years ago we met again, which was weird. I was so excited to see him again and I even invited him to my Sweet 16. He was so excited and then we started talking over the computer. Well, the past couple of days we've been getting along really well and kind of flirting with each other. He says he's my buddy and I'm his buddy.

Two days ago Cliff and I got into this small fight because he said he saw me at his school and I didn't say hi. Well, it wasn't me, it was my friend Betsy! Everyone says that Betsy and I look like twins. So I wanted to bust on him after that and I pretended to be mad. I told him he wasn't my buddy anymore. Well, then he went and talked to Teresa—as if I had been *SERIOUS*! And she told me he asked her if I was really mad at him. I couldn't believe it—but he did.

After that we had a long talk and now we are buddies again but that was a close one. He told me that in order to prove himself he plans to find me and dance with me at Teresa's Sweet 16 this weekend! I was so happy. I can't wait. There's only one problem I see here and that is the fact that all last year Teresa liked him a lot. I heard that he's even gonna be part of her Sweet 16 ceremony.

When Cliff was dating this other girl last year, Teresa was *SOOOO* upset about it, but that was a while ago. I don't know how she feels about it now. And I'm too embarrassed to want to come right out and ask her because I'm really not sure how I feel either. I don't want Teresa to get mad at me just because something *might* happen with me and Cliff. Cuz it *might not.*

Baxter

October 21

Tonight I had a *STUPID* Community Club meeting to go to. It went on forever and I missed the first half of Dawson's Creek, which really pissed me off. As usual, Miss S. was her normal bitchy self and she wasn't satisfied with anything I had to do or say. So *screw it.*

Today I also got a C and a C+ in AP chemistry. *I don't get it.* It just seems that since the beginning of junior year, unlike all my other years in school, I don't get anything anymore. Everyone thinks that just because I'm ranked in the top ten of our class that I'm some kind of super student and I have to live up to that. And whenever I get anything wrong everyone jumps all over me. It's the same always. And lately all I do is get stuff wrong.

Katie

October 21
@ 11 p.m. after the meeting

I feel a lot better now. Not crying. Today when I got my bad chemistry grade, I decided to go for extra help (which I normally can't do because of tennis practice but it was raining so I could). However, my tennis coach informed me that our match was *NOT* canceled and screamed at me and my other friends on the team the minute we got on the bus for the match. I couldn't believe it, but he said that we should always put tennis first and he yelled. I'm sorry, but in my life family comes *way* before tennis and then school and then *maybe* tennis, more likely Community Club.

I think it's because Coach Mayeri just doesn't

understand our needs. He's above it all . . . more worried about driving his expensive car. As a punishment, he told us we couldn't play tomorrow or Friday but we're all pathetically *HAPPY* about that one.

As always, through everything, Brad was there for me—he always is. I was reflecting while I was crying today about the two of us.

While I was lying there sprawled across the cold, hard tile floor of my bathroom, I remembered the last time I had been lying there crying. Thanks to Robert, I became quite familiar with those tiles. I don't know what it is about the bathroom floor. It's my crying place . . . the only place I have ever cried. I guess crying just isn't my image—and if I lock myself in the bathroom no one can see me. When Robert and I were together, I cried every night on that floor for almost 3 months. I used to have to clean up the mascara stains! I remember it was the worst feeling in the world.

Baxter

October 21

This thing with Megan is really bothering me. And I don't know what to do about it. I so want her, but then again I doubt she wants me like that and so everything hurts. It hurts so much. I have never felt this way. I lost my appetite, I am losing sleep. I get so nervous and stupid when I'm around her too.

No one helps make it better. No one knows. I need for them to ask me about it. I don't want to talk about it too much either. I need for them to ask.

Tonight I beeped her. I bet she won't call me back.

My Greatest Asset

<u>Billy:</u>
   Asset: My smooth ways. Ha ha. J/K!! My intelligence.
   Flaw: My insecurities, definitely. I'm not confident and when I try to be I look stupid.

<u>Teresa:</u>
   Asset: I'm the most motivated person I know. Before every hockey game I give my team a motivational speech
   Flaw: I'm such a jealous person and I tend to resent people because of it

<u>Katie:</u>
   Asset: My ability to achieve and get along with everyone.
   Flaw: I know that I can be bossy sometimes and I don't realize it until someone gets upset with me.

<u>Kevin:</u>
   Asset: Def. my Ability to listen And help others.
   Flaw: I'm paranoid And I get overAnxious And wound up. Sometimes I think too ApocAlyptically And intricAtely

My Biggest Flaw

Baxter:
Asset: I trust and believe everyone. If you can't trust someone why should they trust you?
Flaw: I always get my hopes up. I think that everyone is going to surprise me and then I always feel let down.

marybeth:
Asset: I can usually sense what someone is thinking, which is cool.
Flaw: Being a smart-ass. I have a comment about everything and sometimes I just go too far with them.

Emma:
Asset: my personality. I consider myself a rather nice and kind person.
Flaw: I don't know when to say no. I sometimes do things I don't want to because I feel bad saying no to people.

Jake:
Asset: My looks
Flaw: What flaws? Ha ha

Katie

October 22
@ 11:30 p.m.

What a long day—I remember on Sunday they said in the closing speech at church that memories of the retreat will fade and suddenly we'll be back into the real world, and that's exactly what is happening and it makes me so sad. They couldn't have been any more right. Honestly, this has been one of the hardest weeks of my life and I don't even know why . . . nothing major happened. Just a lot of little things.

I think the most painful of all was when Coach Mayeri said I was selfish. Me, of all people! It felt really horrible. With all the 100s of hours I try to spend helping other people and caring about people. That meant nothing at all and went unacknowledged. I don't need to be recognized for helping others but I want it to be noticed. There is a difference.

Like last weekend was *ENTIRELY* devoted to service. This Saturday I am feeding the homeless, doing a fashion show benefit for the nursing home. Selfish, huh? Sunday we're having a huge strategic meeting to discuss Community Club planning from 2 to 6 and I will love every minute of it. I love what I do—if I dedicate my life to service, how can a stupid coach who lives in one of the wealthiest towns in my county call me selfish?

Whatever. I tend to hold grudges and I know it isn't fair to think this way but I will get my revenge. I will make him apologize to me somehow. I'm certainly not apologizing for anything!

We had a rehearsal for the fashion show tonight and I can't wait. I'm wearing three outfits: casual, candy striper, and evening gown. The gown is a long flowing black dress with feathers around the neck. The old people at the home are going to have a good time! *TGIF—THANK GOD IT'S FRIDAY!*

Emma

10/24, 1:03 p.m.

Today was wicked busy. I had to get up at 7 or so and feed breakfast to the homeless. I went with Katie and Marybeth. There was actually only one family we were feeding—a mother and her four children. They were all really young and it was hard to watch them because I was cooking. We made pancakes and french toast and they ate it all up.

After that I had to go to my little brother's birthday party and it was ok except for there were too many little kids there. Some of them were terrible and evil and I just wanted to kill them!

Once again my dad let me drive on the parkway and then on this smaller road by my house. And that was quite an experience. At one point I hit the curb and my dad like went crazy! I hate it so much when he yells at me because then I don't want to drive at all.

Then when I got home, me and my cousin went to the football game. That was totally lousy because the team just didn't play that well this time (my one friend actually got stitches on his arm because it was ripped up pretty bad). It was a bad afternoon overall. I didn't really see anyone I liked at the game. Neither of the 2 Adams were there.

I hope Teresa's birthday party brings me better luck tonight.

Katie

October 24
@ 8:49 p.m.

I got this in my fortune cookie the other day. I hope it's true:

**Your self-confidence shines and makes a
great impression on others.**
Lucky numbers: 5, 14, 20, 25, 33

I had the best time at the fashion show at the nursing home. About 20 of us went over to model outfits. The old folks loved it! Although I am no model on the runway (to say the least—I almost tripped and fell in my heels!) my adviser said that in the way I acted toward everyone I was just like Miss America.

I don't know—it all comes pretty naturally to me. One woman kept reaching out to all the "models" from her wheelchair and everyone just kept blowing her off and even laughing at her. But when I was near her I came to a full stop and leaned over to her, gave her my hand, and knelt next to her. She said, "Pretty girl, please don't leave me. I want to see the pretty dresses. They remind me of my children!" It was so sweet! I just love being able to help like that. None of the old folks walked out either. Everyone stayed for the whole show.

By the way, my friend Jaclyn came home from college this weekend and it was so awesome to talk to her! She's like my older sister in a way—we have a lot in common and she really protected me and helped me through some tough times last year (Robert, grades, etc.). She told me that junior and senior year at JFK is going to feel a little like a prison sentence. Kind of like being 100% ready to move on but unable to move on.

It's true that sometimes I do really feel trapped, but there's nothing I can do. I just have to be patient.

Teresa's party is tonight. Everyone is going to be there. I was supposed to go to this other Sweet 16 across town tonight with Brad, but I think Teresa's is much more important.

Teresa

Dear Diary,

Today I am *SWEET 16*!!!!! Yay! I hate that I have such a late birthday, but oh well! Actually my *actual* birth date was October 19 (at 3:09 p.m.) so I'm officially 16 five days ago. Let's see, that means I get my license in 359 days!! (ha ha)

Tonite I had to write out my candles. What happens is I place 17 candles around my cake and have special people in my life come up and light them. We play music and I talk about why I love them. This is a short version of what I did:

Candle 1: Grandma & Grandpa
(because they are watching over me every day)

Candle 2: Mother (because you are not only my mother but my friend and because you give me the love I need to go on)

Candle 3: Father (because I'm Daddy's little girl no matter what)

Candle 4: Vincent (even though we

176

don't always get along, Vin
is special to me)

Candle 5: Field hockey candle (our team
rocks! We can do anything
"rising up straight to the
top!" because we're chicks
with sticks!)

Candle 6: Hometown boys (Anderson,
Will, and Tommy best pals
from childhood who make me
laugh all the time)

Candle 7: Best girlfriends at
JFK (Katie, Marybeth, and
Emma)

Candle 8: Best boyfriends at
JFK (Manny, Jonny,
Baxter, Kevin, Jake, and
Billy)

Candle 9: In the neighborhood
THE GUYS! (Ivan, Jesse, and
Philip)

Candle 10: In the neighborhood
THE GALS! (Frannie, Lisa,
Barbara, and Uzzie — ha ha)

Candle 11: Senior friends

Candle 12: Good friends

Candle 13: Sherelle (from the day
       we met at field hockey . . .
       until now! I'm just
       jerkin' my chain and
       um . . . I lost my
       beeper, etc. My best
       friend forever . . .)

Candle 14: Wendy (we hated each
       other in 4th grade so
       who knew! You are my
       savior and I would
       perish without YOU!
       You're my best friend
       forever . . .)

Candle 15: Gina (you are my
       sister, my number one,
       and just like our
       parents, our kids will
       be best friends too)

Candle 16: Stephanie (hard to
       summarize a 13-year
       friendship, a friendship
       that will never disappear,

> *my best friend in the*
> *entire world)*
>
> Candle **17** *(for good luck):* Helen
> *(you are my hero and I*
> *look up to you)*

I can't believe the moment to do all this is actually
here! I just know I'm going to cry when I start saying
stuff. I was crying as I wrote them. I'm going to play a
song for each one as I read it out, and most of the
songs just make me cry when I listen to them anyway!

I bought a new blue dress with a low neckline
(that makes me look good) and I got purple tips put
on my nails with a light blue design that actually
matches the decorations. Everything must be coordi-
nated . . . I want it all to be perfect!!! I'm also planning to wear my hair up with one curly piece coming
down, and I have my mom's friend ready to video-
tape. I hope everything runs smoothly! I printed out a
guest list that my dad has so he can make sure no one
comes in that's not invited. And there's a box wrapped
in paper for people to drop their cards in.

I think it may be the best day of my life.

And I even have an awesome horoscope, which
totally describes today (maybe this one will happen
for real):

This birthday season will be one to remem-
ber. With the sun, Mercury, and your ruler

Venus in your sign, you are seriously shining. Sure, you might shock a few friends and admirers, but you're looking cool and talking smart and having a ball just being you. No wonder friendships were never so good! You're a total guy magnet. Soon you'll be deep-down happy too.

Everything about that is sooooo true, except maybe the guy magnet part, which wasn't true before either.

Billy

10-24

Tonight I went to Teresa's thing for her Sweet 16 and almost everyone was there. She told me I could bring Blair D. no problem but I blew it off. I don't know why everyone's birthday has to be so huge. I mean, it was an ok party I guess if you're into that kind of thing. I'm not. Of course I was happy for T. because she looked real nice and all the guys there were saying that. She asked me to light up one of the candles on her cake, so I went up and did it. Actually I spent most of the time with Bax and Jake and Kev because no one I know on the team was really around. We laughed a lot at some of the other goons in the room. I'm real tired now.

180

Emma

10/25, 5:33 p.m.

Last night was Teresa's Sweet 16 party and I had a really good time because everyone was there, but mostly because I saw Cliff there. Yeah! He found me like he said he would and we are still buddies. It was so cute. There was this other DJ there too and he told me that Scott said hi from California and actually his e-mail hasn't been working, which is why he hadn't written or anything yet. That also made me really happy.

Maybe things are working out. I feel a little better now. Before everyone left the party, this kid Justin tried to grab my butt and I slammed into Cliff, so he teased me about it. When I came home the first thing I did was go online to talk to Cliff some more and we were kind of flirting a little. He told me his phone number and I gave him my phone number and he said he would call me tomorrow, which is actually today. I already talked to him twice today and he said he would call me later, after he got back from skating. I hope he calls me one more time. I think I really like him. I dunno though. Maybe I do and maybe I don't really. We'll see.

Of course first I have to get rid of stupid Adams 1 & 2 because they are *BOTH* pissing me off. When Adam M. calls me now I tell him I'll call back and then he calls me again like 10 minutes later and wants to go do stuff. That bothers me. He knows I don't want a relationship and he keeps pushing it anyway. I won't take this stupid shit. And then Adam F. keeps bugging Marybeth to ask for information about me. I'm just going to tell her to tell him how I really feel. Maybe he'll listen if she's the one who says it. I feel bad, but what am I supposed to do? Besides, I don't really like either of them anyway because now I'm starting to like Cliff.

It's strange that most of my friends don't know anything about Cliff. I haven't told them anything and I'm not sure that I will. I also don't know what to do about Teresa because I think maybe she still has some feelings for him. I just don't want her to get mad if something happens between him and me.

Jake

October 25

Last night I went to Teresa's Sweet 16 party and it was definitely a bumpin' party. Especially since Claudia was there and suddenly I wasn't nervous at all. She looked so hot. Before, she hadn't been talking to me because of her needing time, but we talked last night and kind of settled things, and I hope everything works itself out. Then I ripped it up on the dance floor—she loves watching me dance.

Everything around me just seems so much cooler since Kevin got his license. (I can only guess what happens when I get mine!!!) From now on Kevin and me are going to be driving to school together every morning. And all last week we drove around. We went to get his car inspected, went driving to the school, and got gas. It is so good to be in the car with just the two of us like that! Last night after the party Kevin and I went over to hang at Baxter's house for the rest of the night. We played Nintendo 64 and Trivial Pursuit all night until like 4 in the morning. Then when we woke up we ate breakfast and played air hockey and Baxter pulled out this porno that he has hidden. I swear he knows every part of it. Unfortunately I slept later than I wanted to, so I missed my lacrosse practice.

I am *SO READY* for lacrosse season to begin. And this week I'm also starting my job working for this promotion agency in town where you go to different food stores and give out free samples of food. I need to make some cash and it should come in handy over the holidays especially. Tuesday I'll be working at a Super Emporium in the next town over. I know it will be even more fun than usual since Kevin's gonna work it with me and we can drive there together. Plus I'm kind of glad I'll be out of the house more. Maybe it will take my mind off my dad.

Oh, last nite I hooked with Teresa just for a minute after her party. I almost forgot! It was pretty much a non-event since it was only for like two seconds. It was just a hookup and nothing more. Besides, all I could think about was Claudia. The whole time I was kissing Teresa, I was thinking that I was kissing Claudia. Hey, but that's ok because Teresa knows how I feel.

Teresa

10/25
very very late on the day after the PARTY!
Dear Diary,

Last nite was like the best time in the whole wide world! I was nervous at first like maybe some people wouldn't show up. I was pacing and kept checking my hair and makeup. But soooo many people showed up! Basically I was greeting people as they came in and then a group of guys showed up in shorts and tee-shirts who weren't invited, so we kicked them out, and then the DJ played a song just for my mom. She is so awesome! We were both crying!

Everyone loved the music the DJ played (especially Kevin and Jake, who were cracking me up!). Kevin looked pretty cute, actually. Everyone loved the subs too (they were *huge*) and had a good time.

After the candle lighting ceremony, the rest of the night went by so fast! Before I knew it everyone was saying goodbye! I counted up the money when I got home too and I made out pretty good for the 125 people who came! These memories will stay in my heart forever.

In fact, now that I'm 16—and I look back on 15, it was absolutely the *WORST* year of my life. Last night, with all my friends and family around me, I felt hopeful. I feel it a little more right now. Truthfully, I did feel a little left out by people who were all coupled and stuff. God, I could relive the party forever though! And I don't even feel tired right now, which is very strange considering how late it is (I don't know exactly but I know it's very late).

The only thing that I'm actually a little mad about from my party is my friend Stephanie. Here's what happened. Steph actually left my party in the middle—and she didn't even say goodbye to me or anyone! I was so mad! My #1 rule = you don't give up on your girlfriends *ever* for a guy. And of course Steph left with her boyfriend. Well, excuse me.

I don't really know what to say to her about it. It hurts a lot because I always thought that no matter *what* else happened, she would be the one I could turn to for *anything* no matter what. I could trust my life with her. Sounds too good to be true? Well, it is. I barely talk to her anymore. Since she got a boyfriend and has been together with him for over a year, she has basically dropped all of her friends, including me . . . after 13 years of growing up together. It's so hard for me because I thought of all people she would never leave me. Wrong! It's kinda scary. I thought she was the person who would always be there for me no matter what, and now what? Our friendship has basically withered up and is falling apart. Katie says all the time that you can *never* pick a boyfriend or girlfriend over your friends. She is *RIGHT*!!!

Now you can see why I hate guys, right? And I think now that with everything that happened with Stephanie that friendship is totally overrated. No one can really be your best friend for *life*.

I guess for now I'll just keep hanging with my friends, going dancing with the rest of the gang, meeting new hot guys, and just having fun. I just need to hang out with different kinds of people. I feel like it's sooooo important to learn that not everything is what it seems on the outside. Like a lot of people think for whatever reason that I'm some kind of a bitch, but the truth is I'm the most sensitive and emotional person. People can be so wrong sometimes, but what are you supposed to do?

I guess I shouldn't worry so much about friends or boyfriends. Things are decent so far, and *of course* my Sweet 16 was soooooo excellent, so what am I complaining about? God, I am so selfish that I would just ramble on like this after my family and friends threw me the best party of my entire life. I have no right to feel bad. Get over it! I'd better get some sleep now. It's tomorrow already!

Kissing, etc. Kissing, etc.

Jake:

kissing is great. First of all a hookup is just a hookup and it does not always mean that you have to call the girl the next morning, but it's nice. I miss kissing some girls and some girls I could have just passed on, but it was just a hookup so it was no big deal.

Marybeth:

It's better not to kiss a guy like the first time you hang out. If it's something you won't let him have right away, he'll have a greater desire for it. If you kiss a guy at a party or something there's nothing wrong with that only there's no way you can count on a relationship from it.

Katie:

Having a boyfriend is really nice because it feels like someone is solely concerned with you. I'm in favor of holding hands, hugging, and short pecks in public. But I can't see groping each other in the middle of the street. It's important to be somewhere private.

Emma:

I really don't think it's that big a deal when people kiss. It doesn't have to mean there's some kind of sexual thing happening. Like when you see other people kissing you may assume they're going out but that's not always true. I've kissed guys and they are just my friends. Like the other day this kid I was hanging out with kissed me. It just happened.

Kevin:

I will kiss someone in public but won't take it any further than that no way cuz it's way better and more romantic in private. But hey, if someone else

wAnts to get nAsty out in the
open I don't reAlly cARe much.
Once me And some friends were At
A club And in the coRneR this guy
wAs totAlly mAking out w/ this
chick AgAinst A wAll but I reAlly
didn't cARe—I meAn it's not like
I went And threw up oR Anything.

Baxter:

I really don't know jack about this stuff. I fall
in love all the time, but that's because I wear my
heart on my sleeve. And even though I fall in love
doesn't mean I've ever been loved in return. The
truth is I've never been in a serious relationship so I
don't know what it's like having someone to kiss
whenever I want.

Billy:

I think that hookups are BS. They're fun,
but nothing comes of them except trouble.
You kiss a girl and suddenly she thinks you're

together and then her friends all call and hassle you. It's crazy.

Teresa:

Okay, kissing is definitely awesome, but it's not everything. I've kissed some guys that I don't care about and believe me it was not something I enjoyed. But then, when I've kissed people I care about, the kiss was _awesome_! I don't think that kissing means that 2 people are together in any way. It just means that those 2 people shared something special. Whether it happens after that is all based on fate. . . .

Baxter

October 26

Saturday was Teresa's Sweet 16 party and it was fun except for a few things like . . . Megan!

Now I really really like her, but at the party it seemed like she ignored me completely. Every time I nervously tried to talk to her she would give short answers. And then came the bombshell. All night I was too afraid to ask her to dance but everyone told me not to be a wuss and ask her, so I finally did. And she said *"NO."* Not, "I don't feel like it." She said *"NO."* That really broke my heart.

Everyone said that she's still really upset because her cousin died in this really tragic car accident or something this year, and I guess that little things supposedly remind her of him. But still, doesn't she understand that I just want to be there for her? Why won't she let me? Now I'm really depressed.

Emma

10/26, 5:40 p.m.

I talked to Cliff last night! We talked online *and* on the phone! I was too tired from typing so then I asked him to call me up and he did. We talked for over an hour. We may hang out one night next weekend. We'll see. If we hook up, I would be so happy, but I don't want to push it.

Today this stupid sophomore Alexis was giving me dirty looks in the hallway. She's just jealous because I was wearing this guy Devin's football jersey and she wants to wear it. I know for a fact that she really likes him but he does *not* like her. Well—she can't have him! And if Alexis gives me one more dirty look I will beat the crap out of her. Marybeth even saw her giving me stares. The worst part is that Alexis knows I'm looking back at her, so she smiles this annoying smile and that is such a crock of shit because everything she does is all just a *LIE*. Just last night she was actually talking to my sister about me and Devin, and she told my sister that I should back off and go for the other guys! Who does she think she is? Just because she can't wear his jersey and I can does not give her the right to tell me what to do. I love that she is soooo jealous. Plus I have already heard that he may like me anyway—so there. It would be pretty funny if he did since he's so tall and I'm so short. When we were at a party once, we danced and I had to put my arms around his waist.

xoxoxoxoxxoxoxo

Baxter

October 27

AP chem is giving me nothing but problems. I just can't get it. No matter how much I study, which feels like it's all the time, it doesn't help. And that same problem has been happening with a lot of subjects. It seems like everything is caving in on me and I don't have time to rebuild the wall. I have never felt so lost or stupid as I do right now. Everyone says it will get better so it's something to look forward to.

Here's the thing: I'm supposed to be the happy one. I'm supposed to be the happy friend, the one everyone laughs at. But now I'm not. School is not fun anymore. Nothing is. It just sucks. And no matter how hard I try it doesn't seem to work out.

Emma

10/29 7:31 p.m.

I talked to Cliff again last night. It was his birthday and I sent him one of those online birthday cards with a cute teddy bear and hearts. He asked me what I was doing and I said nothing and he said he was doing nothing too and that we should do nothing together sometime. *HOW CUTE IS THAT!?* Today during sixth period I was also talking to my buddy Roger and he is super good friends with Cliff, and he said he thinks Cliff and I should hang out more. Anyway, the coolest thing of all is that Cliff told me I was the first one to wish him happy birthday. He said he felt special. It was cute.

Yesterday I saw that sophomore Alexis again and she wouldn't even *LOOK* at me. She knows better, right? I swear I will kick her ass if she stares at me that way again. I was talking to Devin in history and he said the doctors say he can't play football this Saturday because of his neck. But it's ok if I keep wearing his jersey, even though it's like down to my ankles. It looks better on me than it ever would on Alexis.

I'm waiting to go to church for a retreat meeting. I have to make a speech and mine sucks. I called up Marybeth to read it to her and ask her what she thought of it and she told me what she *REALLY* thought. I was crying I was so upset. She said she felt bad tearing it up like she did, but I'm glad she did rather than the leader telling me it sucked in front of 20 other kids. It is so awesome to have a friend like Marybeth. I really look up to her. She will *always* tell you like it is even if you don't want to hear it. She helped me rewrite the speech but I'm still nervous. I hate talking in front of people worse than *anything* in the world. I get so nervous.

Hey, I got my nails done and they look cute—red with a white design.

10:08 p.m., later on

The meeting is over and I'm back now and it went pretty good. The only comment made about my new speech was that maybe I should add a little more to it. What a relief. Right now I'm on the phone with Adam F. and we are like not talking, which is bad. I want to get off the phone right *NOW*! When will he get the hint? Adam M. called me too and I lied and said I was doing my homework. He is like a year younger than me anyhow and I don't really want to be involved with a baby. Both of these guys are just so annoying now, I can't stand it anymore. I just told Adam F. I was going to bed so I could hang up and call Cliff.

Baxter

October 29

So College Night was exciting but a little scary too. College seems like it's so close but then again I can't believe I have to leave high school. What will we all do?

Yesterday I found some hope again. Really found it. Megan wore my class ring during *ALL* of lunch. It was great, but eventually she gave it back because it was too big and she said she was afraid she was going to lose it. Since she wore it, no one else has even been allowed to *TOUCH* it. Boy, do I love her.

Oh yeah, I failed my AP chemistry test. Maybe I should go as a loser for Halloween this year. Ha ha ha!

Emma

10/30 12:05 a.m.

Sherelle and Bobby came over tonight—and so did *CLIFF*! It's the night before Halloween and we watched TV. Things went really really good. We like sat on the couch and he had his arm around me and I was lying on him, like leaning on him, which was great because we were watching this scary movie, like Halloween IV or something on cable. I was so excited when he told me that he would be there that I screamed, which is pretty stupid, I know.

Sherelle just called me and said that Cliff told Teresa about coming over. (I didn't tell Teresa yet because I didn't want to hurt her feelings. I still don't know how she feels about him.) I hope she doesn't talk shit about me. She really has no reason to be mad because there is nothing going on between me and Cliff yet anyway. I just don't want her to be telling him or anyone stuff behind my back. I don't think Teresa would, but I'm not sure. I think she has it in her. I mean, me and Teresa used to be like best friends but we aren't anymore. We don't talk on the phone or really hang out so how am I supposed to know what she would or wouldn't do? I'm really confused about what to do or think. I'm starting to like him and I won't let her ruin it for me. So from now on I'm just going to act like nothing is wrong, but keep my guard up and the minute someone says something to me about Teresa getting in my business with Cliff I am going OFF on her! Just be prepared. I hate hate hate people who talk shit about me behind my back. I'm getting so upset right now just thinking about it.

Teresa

Oct 30

Dear Diary,

I'm still on cloud 9 from my party last week. I have never had such an awesome time. I just got the pictures back and everyone looks so good. There's this one shot of me and Kevin and Jake that's pretty cute. Anyway, I was reading my horoscope from the newspaper this morning and it says *LIBRA'S MOTTO IS, "I CONNECT,"* which is true about me. I really *do* like to connect to everything and everyone. There's also this formula in Teen this month for figuring out my destiny number (it sounded pretty cool) so I tried to figure out mine (it's something like month plus date and year and all that). Anyway, mine comes out to 1. So the fortune for #1 for November (as in next month) says:

> **Think of Mars, the planet that gets things going. You know how to get what you want and need to survive—no wonder you succeed at life. Having a good time is very important—but it's got to be your good time and no one else's. You love to begin new projects, explore new worlds, and discover new things. Your get-up-and-go dazzles others. One is the number of initiation. Red is lucky for you.**

Kevin

10/30

So it's the day before Halloween and there are a lot of things going on all of a sudden. My car has finally gone to be painted and I am soooo happy. I can't wait to see it. As for Halloween, I'm gonna party all night at a friend's. This Halloween is probably gonna be dull because I have to drive. I mean dull for me—everyone else can get shitfaced but not me, which is totally unfair. I don't know about this whole driving thing because the more that time goes by I'm beginning to feel depressed about it. I feel like some of my friends are taking major advantage of me. I'm disappointed in that. Like I'm not gonna say "No, I don't have a ride for you, *ASSHOLE*," but then again if I'm thinking it anyway why not just say it. It's just my turn right now, I guess.

And oh my God, I couldn't believe this but I found out (I *just* found out) today that Jake hooked up with Teresa at her party a week ago. I can't believe he didn't tell me until now! I'm pissed at him.

OK, I don't know what is going on with them but I do know that Teresa would want something real but doesn't care extremely if nothing comes of it. When I asked Jake what he thought was going on, he said he didn't really know, like it was nothing, just a quick scam. Hmmm. In my opinion they should start going out definitely! They look really good together. I think maybe he still wants Claudia though, and if that's true, Teresa won't do jack with him no matter what.

Oh, on Friday night I went with Adina to her little sister's party. She's like in junior high so it was fun to see all the littler kids there like Jake's younger sister. She's such a pisser! Then we hung out at a friend's house for a while. I felt really super at the end of the night when I drove Adina home and we kissed for soooo long (she has these incredibly soft lips) and I just seriously wish I never ever ever had to leave her.

The other day I was talking to some friends in class and we were remembering the first Friday after the first week of school when we were freshmen. Back then our whole class was all happy and united and it was just sooo different than it is now with all the shit we are putting up with. I sometimes wish it were more like it used to be again, but then I wouldn't be hanging with some of my best buddies from after freshmen year like Mick Lazlo and DJ Jonny or Mick Geffen. They're like my best friends.

It's so odd to look back on everything. I feel weird about it and I'm like really scared. I feel like it's all going way too quick and I *don't* want my life passing me by. At this rate I think it really could if that day in freshman year seems like yesterday. I can't believe I'm a junior now and I can drive and have my own car and shit. Of course I wanna grow and learn but I'm really scared of losing what I have now and even what I may have lost already—but don't know that it's missing yet.

Maybe some incredible thing will happen for Halloween.

I guess that's all for now. Peace out.

real teens

REALITY CHECK!

We want to know about your real-life high school experiences!

Tell us all about:

 your biggest social blunder   your worst enemy

 your secret crush   your biggest thrill

Grand prize winner receives a video camera!

Official Rules:

1. NO PURCHASE NECESSARY. To enter, complete this official entry coupon or hand print your name, address, birthdate, and telephone number on a 3" x 5" card and mail with your completed entry on a separate piece(s) of paper (no more than 500 words) to: REAL TEENS CONTEST, c/o Scholastic Inc., P.O. Box 7500, Jefferson City, MO 65101.

2. Contest open to residents of the USA no older than 16 as of 12/31/99, except employees of Scholastic Inc., its respective affiliates, subsidiaries, respective advertising, promotion, and fulfillment agencies, and the immediate families of each. Contest is void where prohibited by law.

3. Except where prohibited, by accepting the prize, winner consents to the use of his/her name, age, entry, and/or likeness by sponsors for publicity purposes without further notice or compensation.

4. Winner will be selected on or about 10/1/99 by Scholastic Inc., whose decision is final. Odds of winning are dependent on the number of entries received. Winner and their legal guardians will be required to sign and return an affidavit of eligibility and liability release within 14 days of notification, or the prize will be forfeited.

5. Grand Prize: 1 Grand Prize winner will receive a video camera (Estimated retail value: $800)

6. Prize is non-transferable, not returnable, and cannot be sold or redeemed for cash. No substitution of prize allowed, except by sponsor due to prize unavailability. Taxes on prize are the responsibility of the winner. By accepting the prize, winner agrees that Scholastic Inc. and its respective officers, directors, agents and employees will have no liability or responsibility for any injuries, losses or damages of any kind resulting from the acceptance, possession or use of any prize and they will be held harmless against any claims of liability arising directly or indirectly from the prizes awarded.

7. For winner list, send a self-addressed stamped envelope after 10/1/99 to: REAL TEENS Contest WINNERS, c/o Scholastic Inc., P.O. Box 7500, 2931 East McCarty Street, Jefferson City, MO 65101.

YES! Enter me in the REAL TEENS Contest

Name_____ Birthdate_____

Address_____

City_____ State_____ Zip_____

Phone (_____)_____

◣ SCHOLASTIC

RT3